Dart Apprentice:

Beyond the Basics

First Edition

By Jonathan Sande

Dart Apprentice: Beyond the Basics

Jonathan Sande

Notice of Rights

Notice of Liability

Trademarks

ISBN: 978-1-950325-78-8

Table of Contents

Book License 7

Before You Begin 9

What You Need 11

Book Source Code & Forums 13

- About the Authors 16
- About the Editors 16

Acknowledgments 17

Introduction 19

- About This Book Series 20
- Book Sample Projects 20
- How to Read This Book 21

Dart Apprentice: Beyond the Basics 23

Chapter 1: String Manipulation 25

- Basic String Manipulation 25
- Building Strings 30
- String Validation 33
- Extracting text 42
- Challenges 46
- Key Points 46
- Where to Go From Here? 47

Chapter 2: Anonymous Functions 49

- Functions as Values 49
- Higher-Order Functions With Collections 51
- Callback Functions 61
- Closures and Scope 69
- Challenges 71

Key Points.......... 72

Chapter 3: Inheritance.......... 73

Creating Your First Subclass.......... 74
Overriding Parent Methods.......... 77
Multi-Level Hierarchy.......... 78
Type Inference in a Mixed List.......... 80
Checking an Object's Type at Runtime.......... 80
Prefer Composition Over Inheritance.......... 81
Challenges.......... 83
Key Points.......... 84

Chapter 4: Abstract Classes.......... 85

Creating Your Own Abstract Classes.......... 86
Can't Instantiate Abstract Classes.......... 87
Concrete Subclass.......... 87
Treating Concrete Classes as Abstract.......... 90
Challenges.......... 91
Key Points.......... 91

Chapter 5: Interfaces.......... 93

Software Architecture.......... 93
Coding an Interface in Dart.......... 95
Interfaces and the Dart SDK.......... 98
Extending vs Implementing.......... 98
Challenges.......... 101
Key Points.......... 102
Where to Go From Here?.......... 102

Chapter 6: Mixins.......... 103

Problems With Extending and Implementing.......... 104
Mixing in Code.......... 106
Challenges.......... 107
Key Points.......... 108

Chapter 7: Extension Methods 109

Extension Syntax 110

String Extension Example 110

Int Extension Example 114

Challenges 115

Key Points 115

Chapter 8: Generics 117

Using Generics 118

Creating Generic Classes 119

Creating Generic Functions 126

Generics of a Specified Subtype 130

Challenges 135

Key Points 136

Where to Go From Here? 136

Chapter 9: Enhanced Enums 137

Reviewing the Basics 138

Treating Enums Like Classes 141

Challenges 152

Key Points 153

Chapter 10: Error Handling 155

Errors and Exceptions in Dart 156

Debugging 162

Handling Exceptions 166

Writing Custom Exceptions 171

Challenges 175

Key Points 176

Where to Go From Here? 176

Chapter 11: Concurrency 177

Concurrency in Dart 178

Observing the Event Loop 183

Challenge 187
Key Points 196
Where to Go From Here? 196

Chapter 12: Futures 197
The Future Type 198
Getting the Results 200
Asynchronous Network Requests 203
Creating a Future From Scratch 209
Challenges 214
Key Points 216
Where to Go From Here? 216

Chapter 13: Streams 217
Using a Stream 218
Error Handling 221
Cancelling a Stream 223
Transforming a Stream 224
Creating Streams From Scratch 226
Challenges 232
Key Points 233
Where to Go From Here? 233

Chapter 14: Isolates 235
Unresponsive Applications 236
One-Way Isolate Communication 238
Two-Way Isolate Communication 244
Challenges 253
Key Points 254
Where to Go From Here? 254

Conclusion 255

Book License

Before You Begin

This section tells you a few things you need to know before you get started, such as what you'll need for hardware and software, where to find the project files for this book, and more.

What You Need

To follow along with this book, you'll need the following:

- **Computer**: Most any computer running a recent version of Windows, macOS or Linux.
- **Dart SDK**: A minimum version of 2.18.0 is required.
- **Visual Studio Code**: This book uses Visual Studio Code for the examples, but you can use another IDE if you prefer.

If you don't have access to a computer with the above requirements, it's also possible to run most of the example code in this book by visiting dartpad.dev in your smartphone's web browser.

Book Source Code & Forums

Where to Download the Materials for This Book

The materials for this book can be cloned or downloaded from the GitHub book materials repository:

- https://github.com/kodecocodes/dabb-materials/tree/editions/1.0

Forums

We've also set up an official forum for the book at https://forums.kodeco.com/c/books/dart-apprentice-beyond-basics. This is a great place to ask questions about the book or to submit any errors you may find.

"To the greatest Coder of them all."

— *Jonathan Sande*

About the Authors

Jonathan Sande knows what it's like to bang his head against a wall because his app isn't working. He also understands the all-too-frequent feeling of still being completely lost even with twenty-seven browser tabs open. Once he finally does understand a topic, though, he enjoys writing the explanations and directions he wishes he had had when he started. Online he usually goes by the name Suragch, which is a Mongolian word meaning "student", a reminder to never stop learning. After recently deciding to follow Jesus for real rather than just pretending to, he's still trying to figure out if and how coding fits in.

About the Editors

John Bennedict (JB) Lorenzo is a tech editor of this book. He is a mobile expert currently based in Berlin, but was born in the Philippines, where he began his career in tech. In his free time, he does Latin dancing, calisthenics and traveling. He enjoys experiencing different cultures via food, language, stories and travel.

John Hagemann is an editor of this book. He is a government program and policy analyst, technical writer, and editor, and has worked as a journalist and a writing instructor.

Pablo Mateo is the final pass editor for this book. He is Head of the Onboarding & Mobile Center of Excellence at one of the biggest banks in the world and was also the founder and CTO of a technology development company in Madrid. His expertise is focused on web and mobile app development, although he first started as a creative arts director. He was for many years the main professor of the iOS and Android Mobile Development Masters Degree at a well-known technology school in Madrid (CICE). He has a master's degree in Artificial Intelligence & Machine-Learning and a Certificate in Quantum Computing at MIT.

Acknowledgments

The predecessor of this book was named *Dart Apprentice*, which we later split and expanded into *Dart Apprentice: Fundamentals* and *Dart Apprentice: Beyond the Basics*. The original tech editors for *Dart Apprentice* were **Brian Kayfitz** and **John Bennedict (JB) Lorenzo**. Their comments and suggestions greatly improved the content quality. Some of Brian's recommendations didn't make it into the original *Dart Apprentice* but were influential in designing the structure of the current two-book series. **Chris Belanger** was an editor for the first edition of *Dart Apprentice*, and **Joseph Howard** created a video course that influenced the structure and content of that book.

We would also like to thank **Michael Thomsen** on the Dart Team at Google for reviewing *Dart Apprentice* and giving recommendations for updated content to include in this edition.

Introduction

Dart is a modern and powerful programming language. Google intentionally designed it to be unsurprising. In many ways, it's a boring language, and that's a good thing! It means Dart is fast and easy to learn. While Dart does have some unique characteristics, if you have any experience with other object-oriented or C-style languages, you'll immediately feel at home with Dart.

Many people are learning Dart because of the Flutter UI framework. It was no accident that Flutter chose Dart as its language. The Dart virtual machine allows lightning-fast development-time rebuilds, and its ahead-of-time compiler creates native applications for every major platform. As one of the most versatile languages on the market today, you can use Dart to write anything from command-line apps and backend servers to native applications for Android, iOS, web, Mac, Windows, Linux and even embedded devices.

It's no wonder then that developers across the world have taken notice. Rather than completely rewriting the same application in different languages for multiple platforms, developers save countless hours by using a single language and a shared codebase. This translates to a win for companies as well because they save money without sacrificing speed.

So, welcome!

About This Book Series

In its original form, this book started as a single, 10-chapter volume called *Dart Apprentice*. While writing the second edition, we broke the overly-long chapters into more manageable sub-topics, rearranged the teaching order, expanded the explanations and examples, and added completely new chapters. The original 10 chapters grew to almost 30. We didn't want to overwhelm readers with a massive doorstop but to provide them with a learning path that they could complete in measurable steps. For this reason, we split *Dart Apprentice* into two volumes:

1. ***Dart Apprentice: Fundamentals*** is the first of the two-part series. It covers basic programming concepts like expressions, data types, control flow, loops, functions, classes and collections. Readers who complete this book have reached the upper-beginner level.
2. ***Dart Apprentice: Beyond the Basics***, the book you have here, builds on the concepts you learned in *Dart Apprentice: Fundamentals* and introduces new topics like string manipulation, anonymous functions, inheritance, interfaces, generics, error handling and asynchronous programming. If you complete this book, you can consider yourself a solid intermediate-level programmer in Dart.

Book Sample Projects

The book comes with supplemental material that's available as an online GitHub repository. In each chapter folder, you'll find a folder called **starter** that contains a starter project with an empty `main` function. You can either open this empty project in your editor by going to **File ▸ Open** in the menu, or just create a new project.

In addition to the starter project, chapters will also have **final** and **challenge** folders. You can refer to the **final** folder if you get lost during the lesson. It'll contain the code from that lesson. Likewise, the **challenge** folder will contain the answers to the exercises and challenges from that chapter. You'll learn the most if you don't copy and paste this code but type it yourself.

Exercises

You'll sometimes find exercises in the middle of a chapter after learning about some topic. These are optional but generally easy to complete. Like the challenges, they'll help you solidify what you're learning.

Challenges

Challenges are an important part of *Dart Apprentice: Beyond the Basics*. At the end of each chapter, the book will give you one or more tasks to accomplish that make use of the knowledge you learned in the chapter. Completing them will not only help you reinforce that knowledge but will also show that you've mastered it.

How to Read This Book

Most of the chapters in this book build on the ones that precede it, so you'll find it easiest to understand if you progress through the chapters in order.

For readers coming from *Dart Apprentice: Fundamentals*, you'll learn the most by following along and trying each of the code examples, exercises and challenges as you come to them. The way to learn to code is by writing code and experimenting with it. That can't be emphasized enough.

More advanced readers may want to skim the content of this book to get up and running quickly. If that's you, try the challenges at the end of every chapter. If they're easy, move on to the next chapter. If they're not, go back and read the relevant parts of the chapter and check the challenge solutions.

Finally, for all readers, Kodeco is committed to providing quality, up-to-date learning materials. We'd love to have your feedback. What parts of the book gave you one of those aha learning moments? Was some topic confusing? Did you spot a typo or an error? Let us know at forums.kodeco.com and look for the particular forum category for this book. We'll make an effort to take your comments into account in the next update of the book.

Dart Apprentice: Beyond the Basics

Chapter 1: String Manipulation

By Jonathan Sande

If you came to this chapter hoping to learn how to knit or crochet, you'll have to find another book. In this chapter, you'll learn how to manipulate text by adding and removing characters, splitting and re-joining strings, and performing search-and-replace operations. Another essential skill this chapter will teach you is how to validate user input. **Regular expressions** are a powerful tool for that, and in addition to string validation, you can also use them to extract text. Hold on to your hat because you're about to say goodbye to the land of beginners.

Basic String Manipulation

This section will start with a few easy ways to modify strings. These string manipulation methods are easy because they're built right into the `String` type. Anytime you have a string, they're just one `.` away.

Changing the Case

Strings are case sensitive, which means `Hello` is different than `hello`, which is different than `HELLO`. This can be a problem if you're using email addresses as unique identifiers in your database. Email addresses are inherently *not* case sensitive. You don't want to create different user accounts for `spongebob@example.com` and `SpongeBob@example.com`, do you? And then there are always those users who are still living off memes from the last decade and give you `sPoNgEbOb@eXaMpLe.cOm`. No worries, though. Dart is here to save the day.

Write the following code in `main`:

```
const userInput = 'sPoNgEbOb@eXaMpLe.cOm';
final lowercase = userInput.toLowerCase();
print(lowercase);
```

The method `toLowerCase` creates a new string where all the capital letters are lowercase.

Run that, and you'll get a string your database will thank you for:

```
spongebob@example.com
```

If you wish to go the other way, you can call `toUpperCase`.

Adding and Removing at the Ends

The beginning or end of a string sometimes needs a little work to create the form you want.

Trimming

One common thing you'll want to remove is extra whitespace at the beginning or end of a string. Whitespace can be problematic because two strings might appear to be the same but are actually different. Removing this whitespace is called **trimming**.

Replace the contents of `main` with the following:

```
const userInput = ' 221B Baker St.    ';
final trimmed = userInput.trim();

print(trimmed); // '221B Baker St.'
```

`trimmed` no longer contains the extra spaces at the beginning or end of the string. This works for not only the space character but also the newline character, tab character or any other Unicode-defined `White_Space` character.

Use `trimLeft` or `trimRight` if you only need to trim whitespace from one end.

Padding

In contrast to trimming, sometimes you need to add extra space or other characters to the beginning or end of a string. For example, what if you're making a digital clock? The naive approach would be to form your string like so:

```
final time = Duration(hours: 1, minutes: 32, seconds: 57);
final hours = time.inHours;
final minutes = time.inMinutes % 60;
final seconds = time.inSeconds % 60;
final timeString = '$hours:$minutes:$seconds';
print(timeString); // 1:32:57
```

You need to take the remainder after dividing by 60 to get `minutes` and `seconds` because there might be more than 59 minutes and seconds in some duration, which is true in this case where the total duration is over an hour.

Running the code above gives a result of `1:32:57`. This is reasonable for a digital clock. However, changing the duration slightly will show the problem. Replace the first line above with the following:

```
final time = Duration(hours: 1, minutes: 2, seconds: 3);
```

Rerun your code, and you'll see the new result of `timeString`:

```
1:2:3
```

That doesn't look much like a time string anymore. What you want is `1:02:03`.

Dart is here to the rescue again, this time with the `padLeft` method. You can use `padLeft` to add any character, but in this case, you want to add zeros to the left of numbers less than 10.

Replace the code above with the new version:

```
final time = Duration(hours: 1, minutes: 2, seconds: 3);
final hours = time.inHours;
final minutes = '${time.inMinutes % 60}'.padLeft(2, '0');
final seconds = '${time.inSeconds % 60}'.padLeft(2, '0');
final timeString = '$hours:$minutes:$seconds';
print(timeString);
```

The 2 in `padLeft(2, '0')` means you want the minimum length to be two characters long. The `'0'` is the padding character you want to use. If you hadn't specified that, the padding would have defaulted to the space character.

Run the code again. This time, you'll see the following result:

```
1:02:03
```

That's much better.

As you might have guessed, you can also use a `padRight` method to add characters to the end of a string.

Splitting and Joining

Developers often use strings to combine many small pieces of data. One such example is the lines of a **comma-separated values (CSV)** file. In such a file, each line contains data items called **fields**, which commas separate. Here's a sample file:

```
Martin,Emma,12,Paris,France
Smith,John,37,Chicago,USA
Weber,Hans,52,Berlin,Germany
Bio,Marie,33,Cotonou,Benin
Wang,Ming,40,Shanghai,China
Hernández,Isabella,23,Mexico City,Mexico
Nergui,Bavuudorj,21,Ulaanbaatar,Mongolia
```

The fields in this CSV file are ordered by surname, given name, age, city and country.

Take just one line of that file. Here's how you would split that string at the commas to access the fields:

```
const csvFileLine = 'Martin,Emma,12,Paris,France';
final fields = csvFileLine.split(',');
print(fields);
```

The `split` method can split the string by any character, but here you specify that you want it to split at `','`.

Run that code, and you'll see that `fields` contains a list of strings like so:

```
[Martin, Emma, 12, Paris, France]
```

Note that those are all separate strings now, which you can easily access. You learned how to access the elements of a list in *Dart Apprentice: Fundamentals*, Chapter 12, "Lists".

You can also go the other direction. Given some list of strings, you can join all the elements together using the `join` method on `List`. This time use a dash instead of a comma for a little extra variety:

```
final joined = fields.join('-');
```

Print `joined`, and you'll see the following result:

```
Martin-Emma-12-Paris-France
```

Replacing

Find-and-replace is a common task you perform on any text document. You can also do the same thing programmatically. For example, say you want to replace all the spaces with underscores in some text. You can do this easily using the `replaceAll` method.

Write the following in `main`:

```
const phrase = 'live and learn';
final withUnderscores = phrase.replaceAll(' ', '_');
print(withUnderscores);
```

The first argument you give to `replaceAll` is the string you want to match — in this case, the space character. The second argument is the replacement string, in this case, an underscore.

Run the code above, and you'll see the following result:

```
live_and_learn
```

If you only need to replace the first occurrence of some pattern, use `replaceFirst` instead of `replaceAll`.

Exercises

1. Take a multiline string, such as the text below, and split it into a list of single lines. Hint: Split at the newline character.

```
France
USA
Germany
Benin
China
Mexico
Mongolia
```

2. Find an emoji online to replace `:]` with in the following text:

```
How's the Dart book going? :]
```

Building Strings

You learned about string concatenation in *Dart Apprentice: Fundamentals*, Chapter 4, "Strings", with the following example:

```
var message = 'Hello' + ' my name is ';
const name = 'Ray';
message += name;
// 'Hello my name is Ray'
```

But using the + operator isn't efficient when building up long strings one piece at a time. The reason is that Dart strings are immutable — that is, they can't be changed — so every time you add two strings together, Dart has to create a new object for the concatenated string.

Improving Efficiency With String Buffers

A more efficient method of building strings is to use the `StringBuffer` class. The word "buffer" refers to a storage area you can modify in the computer's memory. `StringBuffer` allows you to add strings to the internal buffer without needing to create a new object every time. When you finish building the string, you just convert the `StringBuffer` contents to `String`.

Here's the previous example rewritten using a string buffer:

```
final message = StringBuffer();
message.write('Hello');
message.write(' my name is ');
message.write('Ray');
message.toString();
// 'Hello my name is Ray'
```

Calling `toString` converts the string buffer to the `String` type. This is like the type conversion you've seen when calling `toInt` to convert a `double` to the `int` type.

Building Strings in a Loop

Typically, you'll use a string buffer inside a loop, where every iteration adds a little more to the string.

Write the following `for` loop in `main`:

```
for (int i = 2; i <= 1024; i *= 2) {
  print(i);
}
```

This prints powers of 2 up through 1024.

Run that, and you'll get the following result:

```
2
4
8
16
32
64
128
256
512
1024
```

Each power of two is printed on a new line. What if you wanted to print the numbers on a single line, though, like so:

```
2 4 8 16 32 64 128 256 512 1024
```

The `print` statement doesn't allow you to do that directly. However, if you build the string first, you can print it when you're finished.

Add this modified `for` loop at the end of `main`:

```
final buffer = StringBuffer();
for (int i = 2; i <= 1024; i *= 2) {
  buffer.write(i);
  buffer.write(' ');
}
print(buffer);
```

In every loop, you write the number to the buffer and add a space. There's no need to call `buffer.toString()` in this case because the `print` statement handles that internally.

Run the code above, and you should see the expected result:

```
2 4 8 16 32 64 128 256 512 1024
```

Here are a few more situations where a string buffer will come in handy:

- Listening to a stream of data coming from the network.
- Processing a text file one line at a time.
- Building a string from multiple database queries.

Exercise

Use a string buffer to build the following string:

```
 *********
* ********
** *******
*** ******
**** *****
***** ****
****** ***
******* **
******** *
*********
```

> **Hint**: Use a loop inside a loop.

String Validation

- Hello, I'm a user of your app, and my telephone number is 555732872937482748927348728934723937489274.
- Hello, I'm a user of your app, and my credit card number is `Pizza`.
- Hello, I'm a user of your app, and my address is `'; DROP TABLE users; --`.

You should never trust user input. It's not that everyone is a hacker trying to break into your system — though you need to be on your guard against that, too — it's just that a lot of the time, innocent users make simple typing mistakes. It's your job to make sure you only allow data that's in the proper format.

Verifying that user text input is in the proper form is called **string validation**. Here are a few common examples of string data you should validate:

- Telephone numbers
- Credit card numbers
- Email addresses
- Passwords

Even though some of these are "numbers", you'll still process them as strings.

Checking the Contents of a String

The `String` class contains several methods that will help you validate the contents of a string. To demonstrate that functionality, write the following line in `main`:

```
const text = 'I love Dart';
```

You can check whether that string begins with the letter `I` using `startsWith`. Add the following line at the end of `main`:

```
print(text.startsWith('I')); // true
```

`startsWith` returns a Boolean value, which is `true` in this case. Verify that by running the code.

Similarly, you can use `endsWith` to check the end of a string:

```
print(text.endsWith('Dart')); // true
```

This is also `true`.

And if you want to check the middle of a string, use `contains`:

```
print(text.contains('love'));    // true
print(text.contains('Flutter')); // false
```

These examples are all very nice, but how would you verify that a phone number contains only numbers or a password contains upper and lowercase letters, numbers and special characters?

One possible solution would be to loop through every character and check whether its code unit value falls within specific Unicode ranges.

32		48	0	64	@	80	P	96	`	112	p
33	!	49	1	65	A	81	Q	97	a	113	q
34	"	50	2	66	B	82	R	98	b	114	r
35	#	51	3	67	C	83	S	99	c	115	s
36	$	52	4	68	D	84	T	100	d	116	t
37	%	53	5	69	E	85	U	101	e	117	u
38	&	54	6	70	F	86	V	102	f	118	v
39	'	55	7	71	G	87	W	103	g	119	w
40	(	56	8	72	H	88	X	104	h	120	x
41	)	57	9	73	I	89	Y	105	i	121	y
42	*	58	:	74	J	90	Z	106	j	122	z
43	+	59	;	75	K	91	[	107	k	123	{
44	,	60	<	76	L	92	\	108	l	124	|
45	-	61	=	77	M	93	]	109	m	125	}
46	.	62	>	78	N	94	^	110	n	126	~
47	/	63	?	79	O	95	_	111	o	127	DEL

Unicode characters in the range 32-127

For example, an uppercase letter must fall within the Unicode range of 65-90, a lowercase letter within 97-122, a number within 48-57 and special characters within other ranges, depending on the specific characters you want to allow.

Checking every character like this would be tedious, though. There's an easier way, which you'll learn about in the next section.

Regular Expressions

Regular expressions, sometimes called **regex**, express complex matching patterns in an abbreviated form. Most programming languages support them, and Dart is no exception. Although there are some syntax variations between languages, the differences are minor. Dart shares the same syntax as regular expressions in JavaScript.

Matching Literal Characters

Use the `RegExp` class to create a regex matching pattern in Dart.

Write the following in `main`:

```
final regex = RegExp('cat');
```

There are a few ways you can use this pattern. One is to call the `hasMatch` method like so:

```
print(regex.hasMatch('concatenation')); // true
print(regex.hasMatch('dog'));           // false
print(regex.hasMatch('cats'));          // true
```

`hasMatch` returns `true` if the regex pattern matches the input string. In this case, both `concatenation` and `cats` contain the substring `cat`, so these return `true`, whereas `dog` returns `false` because it doesn't match the string literal `cat`.

An alternative method to accomplish the same task would be to use the `contains` method on `String` like you did earlier:

```
print('concatenation'.contains(regex)); // true
print('dog'.contains(regex));           // false
print('cats'.contains(regex));          // true
```

The results are the same.

Matching string literals has limited use. The power of regular expressions is in the special characters.

Matching Any Single Character

Regular expressions use special characters that act as wildcards. You can use them to match more than just literal characters.

The `.` dot character, for example, will match any single character.

Try the following example:

```
final matchSingle = RegExp('c.t');

print(matchSingle.hasMatch('cat')); // true
print(matchSingle.hasMatch('cot')); // true
print(matchSingle.hasMatch('cut')); // true
print(matchSingle.hasMatch('ct'));  // false
```

Because the `.` matches any single character, it will match the a of `cat`, the o of `cot` and the u of `cut`. This gives you much more flexibility in what you match.

The regex pattern `c.t` didn't match the string `ct` because `.` always matches one character. If you want to also match `ct`, use the pattern `c.?t`, where the `?` question mark is a special regex character that optionally matches the character before it. Because the previous character is `.`, the pattern `.?` matches one *or* zero instances of any character.

Look at the modified example that uses `c.?t`:

```
final optionalSingle = RegExp('c.?t');

print(optionalSingle.hasMatch('cat')); // true
print(optionalSingle.hasMatch('cot')); // true
print(optionalSingle.hasMatch('cut')); // true
print(optionalSingle.hasMatch('ct'));  // true
```

This time all the inputs match.

Matching Multiple Characters

Two special characters enable you to match more than one character:

- `+`: The plus sign means the character it follows can occur *one* or more times.
- `*`: The asterisk means the character it follows can occur *zero* or more times.

Write the following examples to see how they work:

```
final oneOrMore = RegExp('wo+w');
print(oneOrMore.hasMatch('ww'));        // false
print(oneOrMore.hasMatch('wow'));       // true
print(oneOrMore.hasMatch('wooow'));     // true
print(oneOrMore.hasMatch('woooooooow')); // true

final zeroOrMore = RegExp('wo*w');
print(zeroOrMore.hasMatch('ww'));        // true
print(zeroOrMore.hasMatch('wow'));       // true
```

```
print(zeroOrMore.hasMatch('wooow'));      // true
print(zeroOrMore.hasMatch('wooooooow')); // true
```

o+ matched o, ooo and ooooooo but not the empty space between the w's of ww. On the other hand, o* matched everything, even the empty space.

If you want to allow multiple instances of *any* character, combine . with + or *. Write the following example:

```
final anyOneOrMore = RegExp('w.+w');

print(anyOneOrMore.hasMatch('ww'));        // false
print(anyOneOrMore.hasMatch('wow'));       // true
print(anyOneOrMore.hasMatch('w123w'));     // true
print(anyOneOrMore.hasMatch('wABCDEFGw')); // true
```

Here you use the combination .+ to match o, 123 and ABCDEFG.

Matching Sets of Characters

The . regex will match any character, but it's often useful to match a limited set or range of characters. You can accomplish that using [] square brackets. Only the characters you put inside the square brackets will be used to find a match.

```
final set = RegExp('b[oa]t');

print(set.hasMatch('bat'));  // true
print(set.hasMatch('bot'));  // true
print(set.hasMatch('but'));  // false
print(set.hasMatch('boat')); // false
print(set.hasMatch('bt'));   // false
```

The set [ao] matches one a or one o but not both.

You can also specify ranges inside the brackets if you use the – dash character:

```
final letters = RegExp('[a-zA-Z]');

print(letters.hasMatch('a'));  // true
print(letters.hasMatch('H'));  // true
print(letters.hasMatch('3z')); // true
print(letters.hasMatch('2'));  // false
```

The regex '[a-zA-Z]' contains two ranges: all of the lowercase letters from a to z and all of the uppercase letters from A to Z. There will be a match as long as the input string has at least one lower or uppercase letter.

If you want to specify which characters *not* to match, add ^ just after the left bracket:

```
final excluded = RegExp('b[^ao]t');
print(excluded.hasMatch('bat'));  // false
print(excluded.hasMatch('bot'));  // false
print(excluded.hasMatch('but'));  // true
print(excluded.hasMatch('boat')); // false
print(excluded.hasMatch('bt'));   // false
```

`[^ao]` matches one of any character *except* `a` or `o`.

Escaping Special Characters

What if you want to match a special character itself? You can escape it by prefixing the special character with a \ backslash. However, because the backslash is also a special character in Dart strings, it's usually better to use raw Dart strings whenever you create regular expressions. Do you still remember how to create raw strings in Dart? Prefix them with `r`, which stands for "raw".

```
final escaped = RegExp(r'c\.t');

print(escaped.hasMatch('c.t')); // true
print(escaped.hasMatch('cat')); // false
```

If you hadn't prefixed the regex pattern with `r`, you would have needed to write `'c\\.t'` with two backslashes, one to escape the \ special character in Dart and one to escape the `.` special character in regular expressions.

In the future, this book will always use raw Dart strings for regular expressions. The only reason you wouldn't is if you needed to insert a Dart variable using interpolation. See *Dart Apprentice: Fundamentals*, Chapter 4, "Strings", for a review on string interpolation.

Matching the Beginning and End

If you want to validate that a phone number contains only numbers, you might expect to use the following regular expression:

```
final numbers = RegExp(r'[0-9]');
```

This does match the range of numbers from 0 to 9. However, you'll discover a problem if you try to match the following cases:

```
print(numbers.hasMatch('5552021')); // true
print(numbers.hasMatch('abcefg2')); // true
```

That second one shouldn't be a valid phone number, but it passes your validation check because it does contain the number 2.

What you want is for every character to be a number.

You can use the following regex to accomplish that:

```
final onlyNumbers = RegExp(r'^[0-9]+$');

print(onlyNumbers.hasMatch('5552021')); // true
print(onlyNumbers.hasMatch('abcefg2')); // false
```

The regex `^[0-9]+$` is a bit cryptic, so here's the breakdown:

- **^**: Matches the beginning of the string.
- **[0-9]**: Matches one number in the range 0-9.
- **+**: Matches one or more instances of the previous character, in this case, one or more numbers in the range 0-9.
- **$**: Matches the end of the string.

In summary, the regex `^[0-9]+$` only will match strings that contain numbers from start to end.

> **Note**: The ^ character has two meanings in regex. When used inside `[]` square brackets, it means "not". When used elsewhere, it matches the beginning of the line.

Example: Validating a Password

Here's how you might validate a password where you require the password to contain at least one of each of the following:

- Lowercase letter.
- Uppercase letter.
- Number.

Write the following code in `main` to demonstrate how this would work:

```
const password = 'Password1234';

final lowercase = RegExp(r'[a-z]');
final uppercase = RegExp(r'[A-Z]');
final number = RegExp(r'[0-9]');

if (!password.contains(lowercase)) {
  print('Your password must have a lowercase letter!');
} else if (!password.contains(uppercase)) {
  print('Your password must have an uppercase letter!');
} else if (!password.contains(number)) {
  print('Your password must have a number!');
} else {
  print('Your password is OK.');
}
```

This first checks for lowercase, then uppercase and finally numbers.

Run that to see the following result:

```
Your password is OK.
```

You probably noticed that a short password like `Pw1` would still work, so you'll also want to enforce a minimum length. One way to do that would be like so:

```
if (password.length < 12) {
  print('Your password must be at least 12 characters long!');
}
```

You could also accomplish the same task by using a regular expression:

```
final goodLength = RegExp(r'.{12,}');

if (!password.contains(goodLength)) {
  print('Your password must be at least 12 characters long!');
}
```

The `{}` curly braces indicate a length range in regex. Using `{12}` means a length of exactly 12, `{12,15}` means a length of 12 to 15 characters, and `{12,}` means a length of at least 12 with no upper limit. Because `{12,}` follows the `.` character, you're allowing 12 or more of any character.

> **Note**: Although regular expressions are powerful, they're also notoriously hard to read. When you have a choice, go for the more readable option. In this case, using `password.length` is perhaps the better choice. But that's subjective, and the `goodLength` name is also fairly readable, so you'll have to make that call.

Regex Summary

The table below summarizes the regular expression special characters you've already learned, plus a few more you haven't:

- **`.`**: Matches one of any character.
- **`?`**: Zero or one match of the previous character.
- **`+`**: One or more matches of the previous character.
- **`*`**: Zero or more matches of the previous character.
- **`{3}`**: 3 matches of the previous character.
- **`{3,5}`**: 3-5 matches of the previous character.
- **`{3,}`**: 3 or more matches of the previous character.
- **`[]`**: Matches one of any character inside the brackets.
- **`[^]`**: Matches one of any character *not* inside the brackets.
- **`\`**: Escapes the special character that follows.
- **`^`**: Matches the beginning of a string or line.
- **`$`**: Matches the end of a string or line.
- **`\d`**: Matches one digit.
- **`\D`**: Matches one non-digit.
- **`\s`**: Matches one whitespace character.
- **`\S`**: Matches one non-whitespace character.

- `\w`: Matches one alphanumeric character. Same as `[a-zA-Z0-9_]`.
- `\W`: Matches one non-alphanumeric character.
- `\uXXXX`: Matches a Unicode character where XXXX is the Unicode value.

This list isn't exhaustive, but it should get you pretty far.

Exercise

Validate that a credit card number contains only numbers and is exactly 16 digits long.

Extracting text

Another common task when manipulating strings is extracting chunks of text from a longer string. You'll learn two ways to accomplish this, one with `substring` and another with regex groups.

Extracting Text With Substring

Start with the following simple HTML text document:

```
<!DOCTYPE html>
<html>
<body>
<h1>Dart Tutorial</h1>
<p>Dart is my favorite language.</p>
</body>
</html>
```

Finding a Single Match

Say you want to extract the text `Dart Tutorial`, which is between the `<h1>` and `</h1>` tags.

Put the HTML file inside a multiline string like so:

```
const htmlText = '''
<!DOCTYPE html>
<html>
<body>
<h1>Dart Tutorial</h1>
<p>Dart is my favorite language.</p>
```

```
</body>
</html>
''';
```

Now, extract the desired text by writing the following:

```
final heading = htmlText.substring(34, 47);
print(heading); // Dart Tutorial
```

The `D` of `Dart Tutorial` is the 34th character in the string, and the final `l` of `Dart Tutorial` is the 46th character. The `substring` method extracts a string between two indexes in a longer string. The start index is inclusive, and the end index is exclusive. **Exclusive** means the range doesn't include that index. For example, if you write `47` as the end index, the last character in the range will be at index `46`. This might seem strange, but it works out well in a zero-based indexing system where the length of the string is also the end index of the final character.

You're now probably asking, "How in the world do I know what the index numbers are?" Good question. The `indexOf` method will help you with that.

Add the following code below what you wrote previously:

```
final start = htmlText.indexOf('<h1>') + '<h1>'.length; // 34
final end = htmlText.indexOf('</h1>');                  // 47
heading = htmlText.substring(start, end);
print(heading);
```

Calling `indexOf('<h1>')` finds where `<h1>` begins in the text, which turns out to be at index `30`. To find the beginning of `Dart Tutorial`, you need to add the length of the `<h1>` tag itself, which is `4`. Adding `30` and `4` gives the start index of `34`. To find the end index, simply search for the closing tag `</h1>`. Because the end index is exclusive, index `47` is exactly what you want.

Run the code again, and you'll see the same result.

Finding Multiple Matches

What if there are multiple headers? In that case, you can provide a minimum start index to `indexOf` as you loop through every match.

Replace `main` with the following example:

```
const text = '''
<h1>Dart Tutorial</h1>
<h1>Flutter Tutorial</h1>
<h1>Other Tutorials</h1>
```

```
''';

var position = 0;
while (true) {
  var start = text.indexOf('<h1>', position) + '<h1>'.length;
  var end = text.indexOf('</h1>', position);
  if (start == -1 || end == -1) {
    break;
  }
  final heading = text.substring(start, end);
  print(heading);
  position = end + '</h1>'.length;
}
```

Here, you use `position` to track where you are in the string. After extracting one match, you move `position` to after the end index to find the next match on the next loop. `indexOf` will only find the first match after the specified position. If no match is found, then `indexOf` will return `-1` and you can stop searching.

Run the code, and you'll see the extracted text:

```
Dart Tutorial
Flutter Tutorial
Other Tutorials
```

Extracting Text With Regex Groups

The other way to accomplish the same objective is to use regular expression groups. These are the same regular expressions you used when validating strings. The only thing you need to add is a pair of parentheses around the part you want to extract.

Using the same `text` as in the last example, add the following code to the end of `main`:

```
// 1
final headings = RegExp(r'<h1>(.+)</h1>');
// 2
final matches = headings.allMatches(text);

for (final match in matches) {
  // 3
  print(match.group(1));
}
```

Here are explanations of the numbered comments:

1. `<h1>` and `</h1>` match literal characters in the text, and `.+` matches everything between them. Surrounding `.+` with parentheses, as in `(.+)`, marks this text as a regex group.
2. The original text has three headings that match the regex pattern, so `matches` will be a collection of three.
3. `group(1)` holds the text from the regex group you made earlier using parentheses. This example only used one set of parentheses. If you had used a second set of parentheses, you could access that text using `group(2)`.

Run the code, and you'll see the text of the three matches printed to the console:

```
Dart Tutorial
Flutter Tutorial
Other Tutorials
```

Challenges

You've come a long way. Before going on, try out a few challenges to test your string manipulation ability. If you need the answers, you can find them in the supplemental materials accompanying the book.

Challenge 1: Email Validation

Write a regular expression to validate an email address.

Challenge 2: Karaoke Words

An LRC file contains the timestamps for the lyrics of a song. How would you extract the time and lyrics for the following line of text:

```
[00:12.34]Row, row, row your boat
```

Extract the relevant parts of the string and print them in the following format:

```
minutes: 00
seconds: 12
hundredths: 34
lyrics: Row, row, row your boat
```

Solve the problem twice, once with `substring` and once with regex groups.

Key Points

- The `String` class contains many built-in methods to modify strings, including `trim`, `padLeft`, `padRight`, `split`, `replaceAll` and `substring`.
- When building a string piece by piece, using `StringBuffer` is the most efficient.
- Always validate user input.
- Regular expressions are a powerful way to match strings to a specified pattern.
- You can extract strings from text with `String.substring` or regex groups.

Where to Go From Here?

Regex in Your Editor

Regular expressions are not only useful for Dart code. You can use them in many editors as well. For example, in VS Code, press **Command-F** on a Mac or **Control-F** on a PC to show the Find bar. Select the **Use Regular Expression** button, and then you'll be able to search powerfully through all of your code:

The example in the image above finds every line that begins with a capital letter.

Combine that with replacement, and you can even use regex groups. Use `$1` in the Replacement field to capture the first group from the Find field.

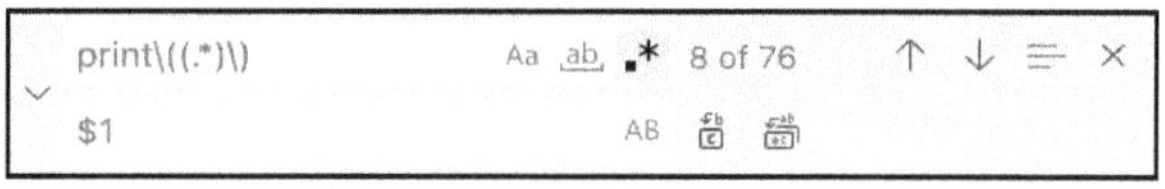

The example in the image above would find something like this:

```
print(text.startsWith('I'))
```

And replace it with the following:

```
text.startsWith('I')
```

This effectively removes the whole `print` statement in a single step!

String Validation Packages

Although any serious developer should know how to use regular expressions, you also don't need to reinvent the wheel when it comes to string validation. Search pub.dev for "string validation" to find packages that probably already do what you need. You can always go to their source code and copy the regex pattern if you don't want to add another dependency just for a single validation.

Chapter 2: Anonymous Functions

By Jonathan Sande

No, **anonymous functions** aren't the secret agents of the Dart world, sneaking around cloak-and-dagger style. They're just functions without names. In fact, they're simply values. Just as 2 is an `int` value, `3.14` is a `double` value, `'Hello world'` is a `String` value and `false` is a `bool` value, an anonymous function is a `Function` value. You can assign anonymous functions to variables and pass them around as arguments just as you would any other value. Dart treats functions as first-class citizens.

The ability to pass functions around makes it easy to perform an action on every collection element or tell a button to run some code when a user presses it. This chapter will teach you how to do all this and more.

Functions as Values

All the functions you saw in *Dart Apprentice: Fundamentals* were **named** functions, which means, well, that they had a name.

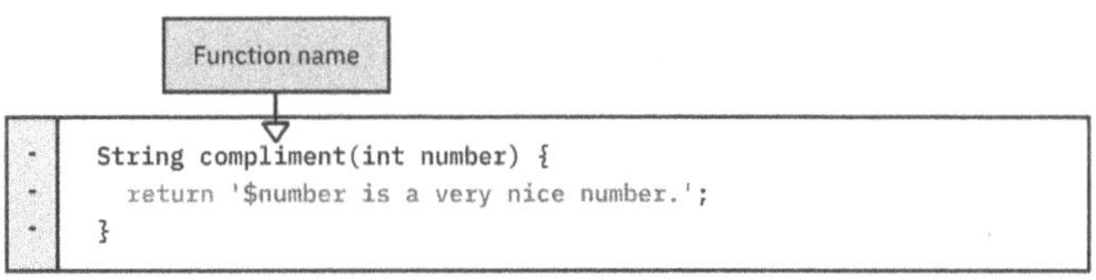

Named function

But not every function needs a name. If you remove the return type and the function name, what's left is an anonymous function:

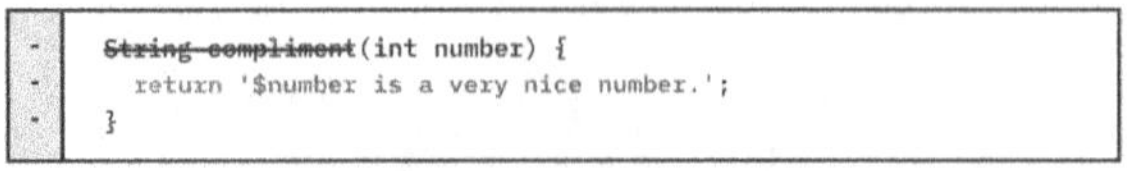

Anonymous function

The return type will be inferred from the return value of the function body — `String` in this case. Removing the name and return type allows you to treat the resulting anonymous function as a value.

Assigning Functions to Variables

By this point, you're already familiar with assigning values to variables:

```
int number = 4;
String greeting = 'hello';
bool isHungry = true;
```

`number` is an `int`, `greeting` is a `String` and `isHungry` is a `bool`. On the right side of each assignment, you have literal values: 4 is an integer literal, `'hello'` is a string literal and `true` is a Boolean literal.

Assigning a function to a variable works the same way:

```
Function multiply = (int a, int b) {
  return a * b;
};
```

`multiply` is a variable of type `Function`, and the anonymous function you see to the right of the = equals sign is a **function literal**.

Passing Functions to Functions

Just as you can write a function to take an `int` or `String` value as a parameter, you can also have `Function` as a parameter:

```
void namedFunction(Function anonymousFunction) {
  // function body
}
```

Here, `namedFunction` takes an anonymous function as a parameter.

Returning Functions From Functions

And just as you can pass in functions as input parameters, you can also return them as output:

```
Function namedFunction() {
  return () => print('hello');
}
```

The return value is an anonymous function of type `Function`. In this case, rather than using curly-brace syntax, you're using arrow notation.

Higher-Order Functions With Collections

Functions that return functions or accept them as parameters are called **higher-order functions.** These originally came from **functional programming**, one of the major programming paradigms, along with object-oriented programming, structural programming and others. Although most people think of Dart as an object-oriented language, it also supports functional programming. You have the flexibility to code in a way that makes sense to you.

One of the most common places you'll use higher-order functions is with collections. You'll often want to perform some task on every collection element. Iterable classes in Dart come predefined with many methods that take anonymous functions as parameters.

The image below shows three examples of higher-order functions. **Mapping** is where you transform every value into a new one. One example would be squaring each value. **Filtering** allows you to remove elements from a collection, such as by filtering out all the even numbers. **Reducing** consolidates a collection to a single value, such as by summing the elements.

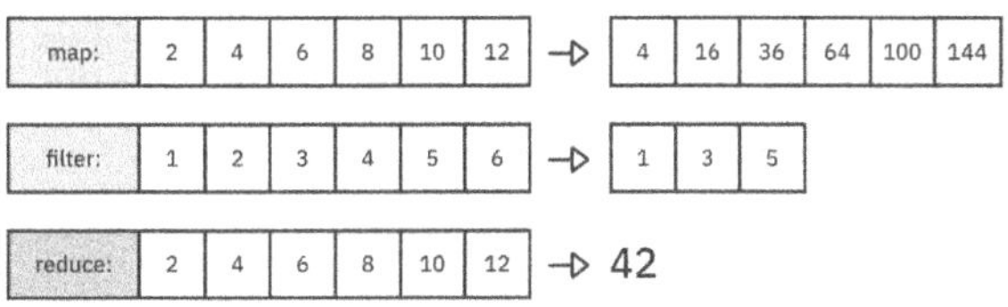

Common higher-order functions

There are many more methods than this small sample, though. Don't worry — you'll discover them in time.

For-Each Loops

`while` loops and `for` loops allow you to iterate using an index. `for-in` loops are convenient for looping over all the elements of a collection without needing an index. Dart collections also have a `forEach` method that will perform whatever task you like on each collection element.

Iterating Over a List

To see `forEach` in action, write the following list in `main`:

```
const numbers = [1, 2, 3];
```

Then, call `forEach` on the list and pass in an anonymous function that triples each number in the list and prints that value:

```
numbers.forEach((int number) {
  print(3 * number);
});
```

All those parentheses and curly braces can get a little confusing. To clarify things, here's the collection with its `forEach` method:

```
numbers.forEach(

);
```

And here's the anonymous function you're passing in as an argument:

```
(int number) {
  print(3 * number);
}
```

The `number` is the current element from the list as `forEach` iterates through the elements. The function body then multiplies that value by three and prints the result.

Run the code, and you'll see the following in the console:

```
3
6
9
```

Because Dart already knows the list elements are of type `int`, you can omit the type annotation for the function parameter. Replace the expression above with the abbreviated form:

```
numbers.forEach((number) {
  print(3 * number);
});
```

This version has no `int` before `number`. Dart infers it.

> **Note**: Choosing to omit the type is a matter of preference. The pro is that your code is more concise; the con is that you can't see at a glance what the type is. Use whatever form you feel is more readable.

Because the anonymous function body only contains a single line, you can replace the curly braces with arrow notation:

```
numbers.forEach((number) => print(3 * number));
```

Note that the *Effective Dart* guide in the Dart documentation recommends against using function literals in `forEach` loops. The standard way to loop over a collection is with a `for-in` loop:

```
for (final number in numbers) {
  print(3 * number);
}
```

This tends to be easier to read.

If, on the other hand, your function is in a variable, then it's quite readable to still use a `forEach` loop:

```
final triple = (int x) => print(3 * x);
numbers.forEach(triple);
```

`forEach` runs `triple` on every element in `numbers`.

Iterating Over a Map

Map collections are not iterable, so they don't directly support for-in loops. However, they do have a forEach method.

Write the following example in main:

```
final flowerColor = {
  'roses': 'red',
  'violets': 'blue',
};

flowerColor.forEach((flower, color) {
  print('$flower are $color');
});

print('i \u2764 Dart');
print('and so do you');
```

In this case, the anonymous function has two parameters: flower is the key and color is the value. Because flowerColor is of type Map<String, String>, Dart infers that both flower and color are of type String.

Run your code to read the output:

```
roses are red
violets are blue
i ❤ Dart
and so do you
```

You're a poet and you didn't know it!

forEach performs a task on each collection element but doesn't return any values. The higher-order methods that follow will return values.

Mapping One Collection to Another

Say you want to transform all the values of one collection and produce a new collection. One way you could do that is with a loop:

```
const numbers = [2, 4, 6, 8, 10, 12];

final looped = <int>[];
for (final x in numbers) {
  looped.add(x * x);
}
```

Print looped to see the squared values:

```
[4, 16, 36, 64, 100, 144]
```

Mapping, however, allows you to accomplish the same thing without a loop. Dart collections provide this functionality with a method named **map**.

> **Note**: This section's map method differs from the Map data type you've studied previously. List, Set and Map all have a map method.

Add the following line of code to main:

```
final mapped = numbers.map((x) => x * x);
```

map produces a new collection by taking the anonymous function that you supply and applying it to every element of the existing collection. In the example above, because numbers is a list of int values, x is inferred to be of type int. The first time through the loop, x is 2; the second time through, x is 4; and so on through 12. The anonymous function squares each of these values.

Print mapped to see the result:

```
(4, 16, 36, 64, 100, 144)
```

Note the parentheses surrounding the collection elements. They tell you this is an Iterable rather than a List, which would have been printed with square brackets.

If you really want a List instead of an Iterable, call toList on the result:

```
print(mapped.toList());
```

Run that, and now you'll have square brackets:

```
[4, 16, 36, 64, 100, 144]
```

It's a common mistake to forget that map produces an Iterable rather than a List, but now you know what to do. The reason List isn't the default is for performance sake. Recall that iterables are lazy. The resulting collection from map isn't computed until you need it.

map gives you a collection with the same number of elements as the original collection. However, the higher-order method in the next section will help you weed out unnecessary elements.

Filtering a Collection

You can filter an iterable collection like `List` and `Set` using the **`where`** method.

Add the following code to `main`:

```
final myList = [1, 2, 3, 4, 5, 6];
final odds = myList.where((element) => element.isOdd);
```

Like `map`, the `where` method takes an anonymous function. The function's input is also each element of the list, but unlike `map`, the value the function returns must be a Boolean. This is what happens for each element:

```
1.isOdd  // true
2.isOdd  // false
3.isOdd  // true
4.isOdd  // false
5.isOdd  // true
6.isOdd  // false
```

If the function returns `true` for a particular element, that element is added to the resulting collection, but if it's `false`, the element is excluded. Using `isOdd` makes the condition `true` for odd numbers, so you've filtered down `integers` to just the odd values.

Print `odds`, and you'll get:

```
(1, 3, 5)
```

As you can see by the parentheses, `where` also returns an `Iterable`.

You can use `where` with `List` and `Set` but not with `Map` — unless you access the `keys` or `values` properties of `Map`.

Consolidating a Collection

Some higher-order methods take all the elements of an iterable collection and consolidate them into one value using the function you provide. You'll learn two ways to accomplish this.

Using Reduce

One way to combine all the collection elements into one value is to use the **`reduce`** method. You can combine the elements any way you like, but the example below shows how to find their sum.

Given the following list, find the sum of all the elements by passing in an anonymous function that adds each element to the sum of the previous ones:

```
const evens = [2, 4, 6, 8, 10, 12];
final total = evens.reduce((sum, element) => sum + element);
```

The first parameter, `sum`, is the accumulator. It remembers the current total as each `element` is added. If you were to print `sum` and `element` on each function call, this would be what you'd get:

```
sum: 2,  element: 4
sum: 6,  element: 6
sum: 12, element: 8
sum: 20, element: 10
sum: 30, element: 12
```

`sum` starts with the value of the first element in the collection, while `element` begins with the second element.

Print `total` to see the final result of 42, which is 2 + 4 + 6 + 8 + 10 + 12.

Try one more example with `reduce`:

```
final emptyList = <int>[];
final result = emptyList.reduce((sum, element) => sum +
element);
```

Run this, and you'll get an error. `reduce` can't assign the first element to `sum` because there's no first element.

Delete that code and continue reading to see how `fold` can solve this problem for you.

Using Fold

Because calling `reduce` on an empty list gives an error, using **`fold`** will be more reliable when a collection has a possibility of containing zero elements. The `fold` method works like `reduce`, but it takes an extra parameter that provides a starting value for the function.

Here's the same result as above, but this time using `fold`:

```
const evens = [2, 4, 6, 8, 10, 12];
final total = evens.fold<int>(
  0,
  (sum, element) => sum + element,
);
```

There are two arguments that you gave the `fold` method. The first argument, `0`, is the starting value. The second argument takes that `0`, feeds it to `sum` and keeps adding to it based on the value of each `element` in the list.

If you were to check the values of `sum` and `element` on each iteration, you'd get the following:

```
sum: 0,  element: 2
sum: 2,  element: 4
sum: 6,  element: 6
sum: 12, element: 8
sum: 20, element: 10
sum: 30, element: 12
```

This time, you can see that on the first iteration, `sum` is initialized with `0` while `element` is the first element in the collection.

Print `total` again to see that the final result is still `42`, as it was with `reduce`.

Now, try the empty list example using `fold`:

```
final emptyList = <int>[];
final result = emptyList.fold<int>(
  0,
  (sum, element) => sum + element,
);
print(result);
```

Run that, and you'll get `0` — no crash with `fold`.

Sorting a List

You've previously learned how to sort a list. For a refresher, though, call `sort` on the `desserts` list below:

```
final desserts = ['cookies', 'pie', 'donuts', 'brownies'];
desserts.sort();
```

Print `desserts`, and you'll see the following:

```
[brownies, cookies, donuts, pie]
```

`sort` put them in alphabetical order. This is the default sorting order for strings.

Dart also allows you to define other sorting orders. The way to accomplish that is to pass in an anonymous function as an argument to `sort`. Say you want to sort strings by length and not alphabetically. Give `sort` an anonymous function like so:

```
desserts.sort((d1, d2) => d1.length.compareTo(d2.length));
```

The names `d1` and `d2` aren't going to win any good naming prizes, but they fit on the page of a book better than `dessertOne` and `dessertTwo` do.

The `compareTo` method returns three possible values:

- **-1** if the first value is smaller.
- **1** if the first value is larger.
- **0** if both values are the same.

The values you're comparing here are the string lengths. This is all that `sort` needs to perform the custom sort.

Print `desserts` again, and you'll see the list is sorted by the length of each string:

```
[pie, donuts, cookies, brownies]
```

Combining Higher-Order Methods

You can chain higher-order methods together. For example, if you wanted to take only the desserts that have a name length greater than 5 and then convert those names to uppercase, you'd do it like so:

```
const desserts = ['cake', 'pie', 'donuts', 'brownies'];
final bigTallDesserts = desserts
    .where((dessert) => dessert.length > 5)
    .map((dessert) => dessert.toUpperCase())
    .toList();
```

First, you filtered the list with `where`, then you mapped the remaining elements to uppercase strings and finally converted the iterable to a list.

Printing `bigTallDesserts` reveals:

```
[DONUTS, BROWNIES]
```

Using chains of higher-order methods like this is called **declarative programming** and is one of the common features of functional programming. Previously, you've mostly used **imperative programming**, in which you tell the computer exactly how to calculate the result you want. With declarative programming, you describe the result you want and let the computer determine the best way to get there.

Here's how you would get the same result as you did using the code above, but imperatively:

```
const desserts = ['cake', 'pie', 'donuts', 'brownies'];
final bigTallDesserts = <String>[];
for (final item in desserts) {
  if (item.length > 5) {
    final upperCase = item.toUpperCase();
    bigTallDesserts.add(upperCase);
  }
}
```

That's not quite as readable, is it?

Exercise

Given the following exam scores:

```
final scores = [89, 77, 46, 93, 82, 67, 32, 88];
```

1. Use `sort` to order the grades from highest to lowest.
2. Use `where` to find all the B grades, that is, all the scores between `80` and `90`.

Callback Functions

When writing an application, you often want to run some code to handle an event, whether that event is a user pressing a button or an audio player reaching the end of the song. The functions that handle these events are called **callback functions**. They're another important use of anonymous functions.

You don't have to do much Flutter programming before you meet a callback function. For example, here's how you might create a `TextButton` in Flutter:

```
TextButton(
  child: Text('Click me!'),
  onPressed: () {
    print('Clicked');
  },
)
```

`TextButton` is the class name, and it has two required named parameters: `child` and `onPressed`. The item of interest here is `onPressed`, which takes an anonymous function as the callback. Flutter runs the code in the callback function whenever the button is pressed.

In the example here, you simply print "Clicked". But the beauty of letting the user supply the callback is that your button can do anything. It could send a message, turn on the TV or launch a nuclear missile. Please don't use it for the latter, though.

Void Callback

The example below will walk you through building a button with a callback method. Because the anonymous function doesn't take any parameters or return a value, it's commonly referred to as a **void callback**.

Implementing a Class That Takes a Void Callback

Write the following class outside of `main`:

```
class Button {
  Button({
    required this.title,
    required this.onPressed,
  });

  final String title;
  final Function onPressed;
}
```

`onPressed` is a field name that will store whatever anonymous function the user passes in.

Create an instance of your `Button` in `main` like so:

```
final myButton = Button(
  title: 'Click me!',
  onPressed: () {
    print('Clicked');
  },
);
```

If you were building a full-fledged `Button` widget, you'd probably call `onPressed` from somewhere within your class. However, because you haven't implemented that for such a basic example, you can just call the function externally as a proof of concept. Add the following line at the bottom of `main`:

```
myButton.onPressed();
```

The name `onPressed` without parentheses is the function itself, whereas `onPressed()` with parentheses calls the function. An alternative way to execute the function code is by calling the `call` method on the function:

```
myButton.onPressed.call();
```

Run your code to check that "Clicked" prints to the console.

Specifying the Function Type

The example above works well, but there's one minor problem.

Create another button like so:

```
final anotherButton = Button(
  title: 'Click me, too!',
  onPressed: (int apple) {
    print('Clicked');
    return 42;
  },
);
```

In this case, you passed in an anonymous function that has a parameter named apple and returns the integer 42. Where does that apple come from? Where does that 42 go? Nowhere. It isn't the void function that your implementation is expecting. If you run that function, you get a runtime crash.

A better approach would be to let users of your `Button` know at compile time that they can only give `onPressed` a void function.

To do that, find your `Button` class and replace the line `final Function onPressed;` with the following:

```
final void Function() onPressed;
```

The `void` ensures users can't supply a return value, and the `()` empty parentheses ensure that they can't give you a function with parameters.

The compiler lets you know that it doesn't like `anotherButton`, so delete that from `main`.

Value Setter Callback

Suppose you wanted to allow the user to run some code every time an update came from within the widget. An example of this is an audio seek bar that notifies about the thumb's horizontal position while a user drags it.

Add the following class outside of `main`:

```
class MyWidget {
  MyWidget({
    required this.onTouch,
  });

  final void Function(double xPosition) onTouch;
}
```

`MyWidget` stores a function that requires an argument when it's called.

Create an instance of `MyWidget` with its callback method in `main` like so:

```
final myWidget = MyWidget(
  onTouch: (x) => print(x),
);
```

Whenever `onTouch` is executed, this function says to print the value of the `x` position.

Normally, you would call `onTouch` internally within the widget as you listen to a gesture detector, but you can call `onTouch` externally as well. Write the following in `main`:

```
myWidget.onTouch(3.14);
```

Because the function caller sets the parameter value, this is a **value setter callback**.

Value Getter Callback

Sometimes your class needs to ask for a value dynamically. In that case, you need a **value getter callback**, which is an anonymous function that returns a value.

Add the following class outside of `main`:

```
class AnotherWidget {
  AnotherWidget({
    this.timeStamp,
  });

  final String Function()? timeStamp;
}
```

In this case, the callback function is nullable, making it optional.

Create a new instance of the widget in `main`:

```
final myWidget = AnotherWidget(
  timeStamp: () => DateTime.now().toIso8601String(),
);
```

Setting the `timeStamp` property allows your widget to call the function anytime to retrieve the value. An **ISO-8601** string is a convenient format when you need to store a time stamp.

As with previous examples, `timeStamp` is normally a function that your widget would call internally, but you can also call it externally:

```
final timeStamp = myWidget.timeStamp?.call();
print(timeStamp);
```

In this case, you can't call the function as `timeStamp()` with parentheses because the function will be null if the user didn't provide one. However, you can use the `?.` null-aware method invocation operator to optionally execute the function using `call()`.

Run the code above to see the time stamp:

```
2022-10-12T14:59:14.438099
```

That's the precise time this chapter was being prepared for publishing.

Simplifying With Tear-Offs

When you have a function, you can either execute the function immediately or hold a reference to it. The difference is in the parentheses:

- **`myFunction()`**: executes the function code immediately.
- **`myFunction`**: references the function without executing the code.

Being able to reference a function by its name allows you to make some simplifications.

For example, add the following class outside of your `main` method:

```
class StateManager {
  int _counter = 0;

  void handleButtonClick() {
    _counter++;
  }
}
```

This class represents a simple state management class that you might use in Flutter.

Now, replace the body of `main` with the following content:

```
final manager = StateManager();

final myButton = Button(
  title: 'Click me!',
  onPressed: () {
    manager.handleButtonClick();
  },
);
```

Pay attention to the anonymous function that you passed to `onPressed`. You'll see many people writing code like this. The author does it all the time. You can do better, though.

The `()` parentheses at the end of `handleButtonClick()` tell Dart to execute this function, but the `() { }` syntax for the anonymous function tells Dart not to execute this function yet. Dart stores it in the `onPressed` property for possible execution later. You've got a command to execute and a command to not execute. These cancel each other out, so you have an opportunity to simplify that syntax.

Find these three lines:

```
onPressed: () {
  manager.handleButtonClick();
},
```

And replace them with this line:

```
onPressed: manager.handleButtonClick,
```

Because `handleButtonClick` doesn't have parentheses after it, it isn't executed right away. This is known as a **tear-off**. You tore the `handleButtonClick` method off and converted it to a function object to be stored in the `onPressed` property. This syntax is much cleaner.

Tear-offs work in other places, too. Say you want to print each element in a list. You *could* do that like so:

```
const cities = ['Istanbul', 'Ankara', 'Izmir', 'Bursa',
'Antalya'];
cities.forEach((city) => print(city));
```

But because the anonymous function and `print` have the same property, `city`, you can use a tear-off instead:

```
cities.forEach(print);
```

Run that to see the names of each of these large Turkish cities printed to the console:

```
Istanbul
Ankara
Izmir
Bursa
Antalya
```

Renaming With Type Aliases

One more way to simplify your syntax is by using **typedef**, which is short for "type definition". This keyword allows you to give an alias to a long type name so that it's shorter and easier to understand.

Take this example:

```
class Gizmo {
  Gizmo({
    required this.builder,
  });

  final Map<String, int> Function(List<int>) builder;
}
```

The type `Map<String, int> Function(List<int>)` is a function that takes a list of integers as input and returns a map of `String`-to-`int` key-values pairs. That's quite complex and hard to read.

Add a type alias for the function outside of `Gizmo`:

```
typedef MapBuilder = Map<String, int> Function(List<int>);
```

`MapBuilder` is the alias for your complex function signature.

Now, you can rewrite your `Gizmo` class like so:

```
class Gizmo {
  Gizmo({
    required this.builder,
  });

  final MapBuilder builder;
}
```

This is much more readable. Flutter takes this approach of giving aliases for many of its callback and builder functions.

You can use `typedef` to rename other types as well. For example, write the following line outside of `main`:

```
typedef ZipCode = int;
```

This doesn't create a new type. Instead, `ZipCode` is just another way of referring to the `int` type. You can observe that in the code below:

Write the following in `main`:

```
ZipCode code = 87101;
int number = 42;

print(code is ZipCode);   // true
print(code is int);       // true
print(number is ZipCode); // true
print(number is int);     // true
```

The purpose of the `is` keyword is to distinguish between types. However, in this case, `is` treats `int` and its alias `ZipCode` exactly the same ... because they're the same.

> **Note**: If you need a new type to store postal codes, you should create a *class* and not a type alias. This will allow you to distinguish the postal code type from `int` and validate its data. For example, you probably wouldn't want to allow numbers like `-1` or `42` to be postal codes.

Exercise

1. Create a class named `Surface`.
2. Give the class a property named `onTouch`, a callback function that provides x and y coordinates but returns nothing.
3. Make a type alias named `TouchHandler` for the callback function.
4. In `Surface`, create a method named `touch`, which takes x and y coordinates and then internally calls `onTouch`.
5. In `main`, create an instance of `Surface` and pass in an anonymous function that prints the x and y coordinates.
6. Still in `main`, call `touch` where x is `202.3` and y is `134.0`.

Closures and Scope

Anonymous functions in Dart act as **closures**. The term closure means that the code "closes around" the surrounding scope and therefore has access to variables and functions defined within that scope.

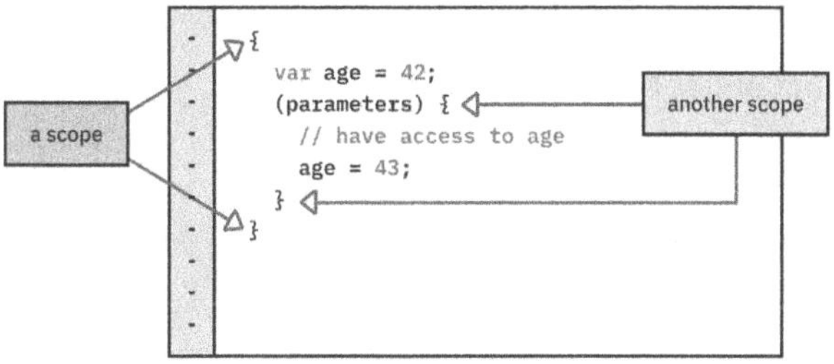

Scope

A scope in Dart is defined by a pair of curly braces. All the code within these braces is a scope. You can even have nested scopes within other scopes. Examples of scopes are function bodies and the bodies of loops.

Closure Example

Write the following in `main`:

```
var counter = 0;
final incrementCounter = () {
  counter += 1;
};
```

The anonymous function that defines `incrementCounter` acts as a closure. It can access `counter`, even though `counter` is neither a parameter of the anonymous function nor defined in the function body.

Call `incrementCounter` five times and print `counter`:

```
incrementCounter();
incrementCounter();
incrementCounter();
incrementCounter();
incrementCounter();
print(counter); // 5
```

You'll see that `counter` now has a value of 5.

A Function That Counts Itself

If you return a closure from a function, that function will be able to count the number of times it was called. To see this in action, add the following function outside of `main`:

```
Function countingFunction() {
  var counter = 0;
  final incrementCounter = () {
    counter += 1;
    return counter;
  };
  return incrementCounter;
}
```

Each function returned by `countingFunction` will have its own version of `counter`. So if you were to generate two functions with `countingFunction`, like so:

```
final counter1 = countingFunction();
final counter2 = countingFunction();
```

...then each call to those functions will increment its own `counter` independently:

```
print(counter1()); // 1
print(counter2()); // 1
print(counter1()); // 2
print(counter1()); // 3
print(counter2()); // 2
```

Admittedly, you probably won't write self-counting functions every day. But this example demonstrated another aspect of the Dart programming language.

In this chapter, you learned a bit about functional programming. In the next chapter, you'll dive into the essentials of object-oriented programming.

Challenges

Before moving on, here are some challenges to test your knowledge of anonymous functions. It's best if you try to solve them yourself, but solutions are available with the supplementary materials for this book if you get stuck.

Challenge 1: Animalsss

Given the map below:

```
final animals = {
  'sheep': 99,
  'goats': 32,
  'snakes': 7,
  'lions': 80,
  'seals': 18,
};
```

Use higher-order functions to find the total number of animals whose names begin with "s". How many sheep, snakes and seals are there?

Challenge 2: Can You Repeat That?

Write a function named `repeatTask` with the following definition:

```
int repeatTask(int times, int input, Function task)
```

It repeats a given `task` on `input` for `times` number of times.

Pass an anonymous function to `repeatTask` to square the input of 2 four times. Confirm that you get the result 65536 because 2 squared is 4, 4 squared is 16, 16 squared is 256 and 256 squared is 65536.

Key Points

- Anonymous functions don't have a function name, and the return type is inferred.
- Dart functions are first-class citizens and thus can be assigned to variables and passed around as values.
- Dart supports both functional and object-oriented programming paradigms.
- Higher-order functions are functions that return functions or accept them as parameters.
- Dart collections contain many methods that accept anonymous functions as parameters. Examples include `forEach`, `map`, `where`, `reduce` and `fold`.
- Chaining higher-order methods together is typical of declarative programming and allows you to solve many problems without the loops of imperative programming.
- Callback functions are anonymous functions that you provide to handle events.
- Tear-offs are function objects with the same parameters as the method you pass them to, which allows you to omit the parameters altogether.
- The `typedef` keyword allows you to rename types so they're shorter or easier to understand.
- Anonymous functions act as closures, capturing any variables or functions within their scope.

Chapter 3: Inheritance

By Jonathan Sande

Do you have your mother's eyes or your father's nose? You weren't built from scratch. You inherited your biological characteristics from your ancestors when their DNA was passed down to you. Likewise, when building classes, you often don't need to start from scratch.

In many situations, you'll need to create a hierarchy of classes that share some base functionality. You can create your own hierarchies by **extending classes**. This is also called **inheritance** because the classes form a tree in which **child classes** inherit from **parent classes**. The parent and child classes are also called **superclasses** and **subclasses** respectively. The `Object` class is the top superclass for all non-nullable types in Dart. All other classes, except `Null`, are subclasses of `Object`.

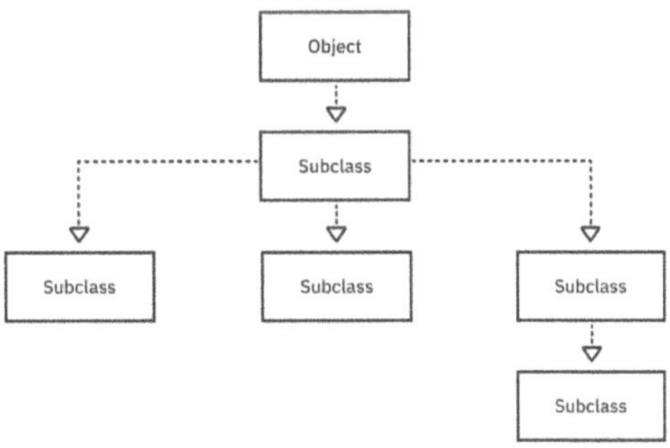

> **Note**: Although there's no named top type in Dart, since all non-nullable Dart types derive from the `Object` type and `Object` itself is a subtype of the nullable `Object?` type, `Object?` can be considered in practice to be the root of the type system.

Creating Your First Subclass

To see how inheritance works, you'll create your own hierarchy of classes. In a little while, you'll make a `Student` class that needs grades, so first make a `Grade` enum:

```
enum Grade { A, B, C, D, F }
```

Creating Similar Classes

Next, create two classes named `Person` and `Student`.

Here's `Person`:

```
class Person {
  Person(this.givenName, this.surname);

  String givenName;
  String surname;
  String get fullName => '$givenName $surname';

  @override
  String toString() => fullName;
}
```

And this is `Student`:

```
class Student {
  Student(this.givenName, this.surname);

  String givenName;
  String surname;
  var grades = <Grade>[];
  String get fullName => '$givenName $surname';

  @override
  String toString() => fullName;
}
```

Naturally, the `Person` and `Student` classes are very similar, since students are in fact persons. The only difference at the moment is that a `Student` will have a list of `grades`.

Subclassing to Remove Code Duplication

You can remove the duplication between `Student` and `Person` by making `Student` **extend** `Person`. You do so by adding `extends Person` after the class name and removing everything but the `Student` constructor and the `grades` list.

Replace the `Student` class with the following code:

```
class Student extends Person {
  Student(String givenName, String surname)
    : super(givenName, surname);

  var grades = <Grade>[];
}
```

There are a few points to pay attention to:

- The constructor parameter names don't refer to `this` anymore. Whenever you see the keyword `this`, you should remember that `this` refers to the current object, which in this case would be an instance of the `Student` class. Since `Student` no longer contains the field names `givenName` and `surname`, using `this.givenName` or `this.surname` would have nothing to reference.
- In contrast to `this`, the `super` keyword is used to refer one level up the hierarchy. Similar to the forwarding constructor that you learned about in *Dart Apprentice: Fundamentals*, Chapter 8, "Classes", using `super(givenName, surname)` passes the constructor parameters on to another constructor. However, since you're using `super` instead of `this`, you're forwarding the parameters to the parent class's constructor, that is, to the constructor of `Person`.

Super Parameters

Rather than manually forwarding constructor parameters to the superclass, you can use `super` plus the parameter name directly. Replace your `Student` class with the following simplified form:

```
class Student extends Person {
  Student(super.givenName, super.surname);

  var grades = <Grade>[];
}
```

Now you're no longer using a forwarding constructor, just directly setting the parameters in the superclass. Super nice, huh?

Calling Super Last in an Initializer List

As a quick side note, if you use an initializer list, the call to `super` always goes last, that is, after any initializers. You can see the order in the following example:

```
class SomeChild extends SomeParent {

  SomeChild(double height, double width, String name)
      : _width = width,         // initializer
      : _height = height,       // initializer
        super(name);            // super

  final double _width;
  final double _height;
}
```

If there are no parameters to pass to the superclass, you don't need to write `super()` because Dart always calls the default constructor for the superclass. The reason that you or Dart always need to make the `super` call is to ensure that all of the field values have finished initializing.

Using the Classes

OK, back to the primary example. Create `Person` and `Student` objects in `main` like so:

```
final jon = Person('Jon', 'Snow');
final jane = Student('Jane', 'Snow');
print(jon.fullName);
print(jane.fullName);
```

Run that and observe that both have full names:

```
Jon Snow
Jane Snow
```

The `fullName` for `Student` is coming from the `Person` class.

If you have a grade, you can only add that grade to the `Student` and not to the `Person`, because only the `Student` has `grades`. Add the following two lines to `main`:

```
final historyGrade = Grade.B;
jane.grades.add(historyGrade);
```

The student `jane` now has one grade in the `grades` list.

Overriding Parent Methods

Suppose you want the student's full name to print out differently than the default way it's printed in `Person`. You can do so by **overriding** the `fullName` getter. Add the following two lines to the bottom of the `Student` class:

```
@override
String get fullName => '$surname, $givenName';
```

You've seen the `@override` annotation before with the `toString` method. While using `@override` is technically optional in Dart, it does help in that the compiler will give you an error if you think you're overriding something that doesn't actually exist in the parent class.

Run the code now and you'll see the student's full name printed differently than the parent's.

```
Jon Snow
Snow, Jane
```

Calling Super From an Overridden Method

As another aside, sometimes you override methods of the parent class because you want to *add* functionality, rather than replace it, as you did above. In that case, you usually make a call to `super` either at the beginning or end of the overridden method.

Have a look at the following example:

```
class SomeParent {
  void doSomeWork() {
    print('parent working');
  }
}

class SomeChild extends SomeParent {
  @override
  void doSomeWork() {
    super.doSomeWork();
    print('child doing some other work');
  }
}
```

Since `doSomeWork` in the child class makes a call to `super.doSomeWork`, both the parent and the child methods run. So if you were to call the child method like so:

```
final child = SomeChild();
child.doSomeWork();
```

You would see the following result:

```
parent working
child doing some other work
```

The parent method's work was done first since you had the `super` call at the *beginning* of the overridden method in the child. If you wanted to do the child method's work first, though, you would put the `super` call at the *end* of the method, like so:

```
@override
void doSomeWork() {
  print('child doing some other work');
  super.doSomeWork();
}
```

> **Note**: To take an example from Flutter, the documentation recommends that when you extend the `State` class and override `initState`, you should place a call to `super.initState()` at the *top* of the method. Conversely, when you override `dispose`, the documentation says you should *end* the method with a call to `super.dispose()`.

Multi-Level Hierarchy

Back to the primary example again. Add more than one level to your class hierarchy by defining a class that extends from `Student`.

```
class SchoolBandMember extends Student {
  SchoolBandMember(super.givenName, super.surname);

  static const minimumPracticeTime = 2;
}
```

SchoolBandMember is a Student that has a minimumPracticeTime. The SchoolBandMember constructor sets the Student constructor parameters by using the super keyword. The Student constructor will, in turn, call the Person constructor.

Sibling Classes

Create a sibling class to SchoolBandMember named StudentAthlete that also derives from Student.

```
class StudentAthlete extends Student {
  StudentAthlete(super.givenName, super.surname);

  bool get isEligible =>
    grades.every((grade) => grade != Grade.F);
}
```

In order to remain eligible for athletics, a student athlete has an isEligible getter that makes sure the athlete has not failed any classes. The higher-order method every on the grades list only returns true if every element of the list passes the given condition, which, in this case, means that none of the grades is F.

So now you can create band members and athletes.

```
final jessie = SchoolBandMember('Jessie', 'Jones');
final marty = StudentAthlete('Marty', 'McFly');
```

Visualizing the Hierarchy

Here's what your class hierarchy looks like now:

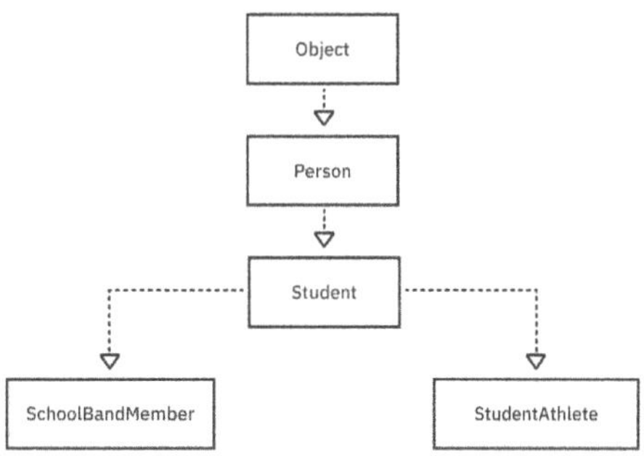

You see that SchoolBandMember and StudentAthlete are both students, and all students are also persons.

Type Inference in a Mixed List

Since Jane, Jessie and Marty are all students, you can put them into a list.

```
final students = [jane, jessie, marty];
```

Recall that jane is a Student, jessie is a SchoolBandMember and marty is a StudentAthlete. Since they are all different types, what type is the list?

Hover your cursor over students to find out.

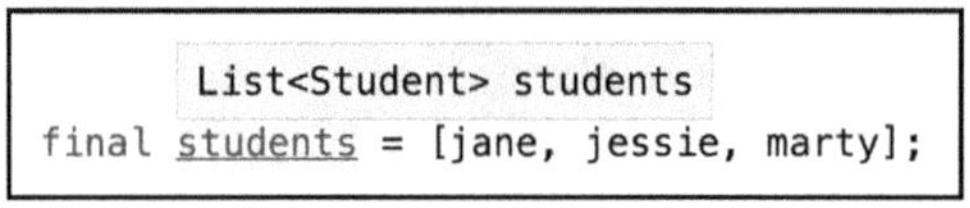

You can see that Dart has inferred the type of the list to be List<Student>. Dart used the most specific common ancestor as the type for the list. It couldn't use SchoolBandMember or StudentAthlete since that doesn't hold true for all elements of the list.

Checking an Object's Type at Runtime

You can use the is and is! keywords to check whether a given object is or is not within the direct hierarchy of a class. Write the following code:

```
print(jessie is Object);
print(jessie is Person);
print(jessie is Student);
print(jessie is SchoolBandMember);
print(jessie is! StudentAthlete);
```

Knowing that jessie is a SchoolBandMember, first guess what Dart will show and then run the code to see if you were right.

Ready? All five will print true since jessie is SchoolBandMember, which is a subclass of Student, which is a subclass of Person, which is a subclass of Object. The only type that jessie is not, is StudentAthlete — which you confirmed by using the is! keyword.

> **Note**: The exclamation mark at the end of is! has nothing to do with the null assignment operator from null safety. It just means *not*.

Having an object be able to take multiple forms is known as **polymorphism**. This is a key part of object-oriented programming. You'll learn to make polymorphic classes in an even more sophisticated way in Chapter 4, "Abstract Classes".

First, though, a word of caution.

Prefer Composition Over Inheritance

Now that you know about inheritance, you may feel ready to conquer the world. You can model anything as a hierarchy. Experience, though, will teach you that deep hierarchies are not always the best choice.

You may have already noticed this fact in the code above. For example, when you're overriding a method, do you need to call `super`? And if you do, should you call `super` at the beginning of the method, or at the end? Often the only way to know is to check the source code of the parent class. Jumping back and forth between levels of the hierarchy can make coding difficult.

Another problem with hierarchies is that they're tightly bound together. Changes to a parent class can break a child class. For example, say that you wanted to "fix" the `Person` class by removing `givenName` and replacing it with `firstName` and `middleName`.

Doing this would also require you to update, or refactor, all of the code that uses the subclasses as well. Even if you didn't remove `givenName`, but simply added `middleName`, users of classes like `StudentBandMember` would be affected without realizing it.

Tight coupling isn't the only problem. What if Jessie, who is a school band member, also decides to become an athlete? Do you make another class called `SchoolBandMemberAndStudentAthlete`? What if she joins the student union, too? Obviously, things could get out of hand quickly.

This has led many people to say, **prefer composition over inheritance**. The phrase means that, when appropriate, you should *add* behavior to a class rather than share behavior with an ancestor. It's more of a focus on what an object *has*, rather than what an object *is*. For example, you could flatten the hierarchy for `Student` by giving the student a list of roles, like so:

```
class Student {
  List<Role>? roles;
}
```

When you create a student, you could pass in the roles as a constructor parameter. This would also let you add and remove roles later. Of course, since Dart doesn't come with the `Role` type, you'd have to define it yourself. You'd need to make `Role` abstract enough so that a role could be a band member, an athlete or a student union member. You'll learn about making abstract classes like this in the next chapter.

All this talk of composition isn't to say that inheritance is *always* bad. It might make sense to still have `Student` extend `Person`. Inheritance can be good when a subclass needs *all* of the behavior of its parent. However, when you only need some of that behavior, you should consider passing in the behavior as a parameter, or perhaps even using a mixin, which you'll learn about in Chapter 6, "Mixins".

> **Note**: The whole Flutter framework is organized around the idea of composition. You build your UI as a tree of widgets, where each widget *does* one simple thing and *has* zero or more child widgets that also do one simple thing. This type of architecture generally makes it easier to understand the purpose of a class.
>
> At the same time, Flutter also makes good use of inheritance. For example, `StatefulWidget` and `StatelessWidget` are both subclasses of `Widget`. The `Widget` class itself is **abstract**, a concept you'll learn about in the next chapter.

Challenges

Before moving on, here are some challenges to test your knowledge of inheritance. It's best if you try to solve them yourself, but solutions are available with the supplementary materials for this book if you get stuck.

Challenge 1: Fruity Colors

1. Create a class named `Fruit` with a `String` field named `color` and a method named `describeColor`, which uses `color` to print a message.
2. Create a subclass of `Fruit` named `Melon` and then create two `Melon` subclasses named `Watermelon` and `Cantaloupe`.
3. Override `describeColor` in the `Watermelon` class to vary the output.

Challenge 2: Composition Over Inheritance

1. Create a `Person` class.
2. Create a `Student` class that inherits from `Person`.
3. Give the `Student` class a list of roles, including athlete, band member and student union member. You can use an enum for the roles.
4. Create some `Student` objects and give them various roles.

Key Points

- A subclass has access to the data and methods of its parent class.
- You can create a subclass of another class by using the `extends` keyword.
- A subclass can override its parent's methods or properties to provide custom behavior.
- Prefer adding behaviors to a class over inheriting behavior from a parent.

Chapter 4: Abstract Classes

By Jonathan Sande

The classes and subclasses you created previously were **concrete classes**. It's not that they're made of cement; it just means that you can make actual objects out of them. That's in contrast to **abstract classes**, from which you can't make objects.

"What's the use of a class you can't make an object out of?" asks the pragmatist. "What's the use of ideas?" answers the philosopher. You deal with abstract concepts all the time, and you don't think about them at all.

Have you ever seen an animal? "Uh, are you seriously asking me that?" you answer. The question isn't "have you ever seen a chicken or a platypus or a mouse." Have you ever seen a generic animal, devoid of all features that are relevant to only one kind of animal — just the essence of "animal" itself? What would that even look like? It can't have four legs because ducks are animals and they have two legs. It can't have hair because rattlesnakes are animals and they don't have hair. Worms are animals, too, right? So there go the eyes and bones.

No one has seen an "animal" in the abstract sense, but everybody has seen concrete instances of things that fit the abstract animal category. Humans are good at generalizing and categorizing the observations they make, and honestly, these abstract ideas are very useful. They allow you to make short statements like "I saw a lot of animals at the zoo" instead of "I saw a lion, an elephant, a lemur, a shark, ..."

The same thing applies in object-oriented programming. After making lots of concrete classes, you begin to notice patterns and more generalized characteristics of the classes you're writing. So when you come to the point of just wanting to describe the general characteristics and behavior of a class without specifying the exact way that class is implemented, you're ready to write abstract classes. In some languages, this generalized behavior is called a protocol, but in Dart it's called an **interface**. You'll learn about that in Chapter 5, "Interfaces". This chapter will prepare you by teaching you the mechanics of creating abstract classes.

Don't be put off by the word "abstract". It's no more difficult than the idea of an animal.

Creating Your Own Abstract Classes

Have a go at working this out in Dart now. Without venturing too far into the fringes of how taxonomists make their decisions, create the following `Animal` class:

```
abstract class Animal {
  bool isAlive = true;
  void eat();
  void move();

  @override
  String toString() {
    return "I'm a $runtimeType";
  }
}
```

Here are a few important points about that code:

- The way you define an abstract class in Dart is to put the `abstract` keyword before `class`.
- In addition to the class itself being abstract, `Animal` also has two abstract methods: `eat` and `move`. You know they're abstract because they don't have curly braces; they just end with a semicolon.
- These abstract methods describe behavior that a subclass must implement. However, they don't tell *how* to implement that behavior. That's up to the subclass, which is a good thing. There are so many ways to eat and move throughout the animal kingdom that it would be almost impossible for `Animal` to specify anything meaningful here.

- Note that just because a class is abstract doesn't mean that it can't have concrete methods or data. You can see that `Animal` has a concrete `isAlive` field, with a default value of `true`. `Animal` also has a concrete implementation of the `toString` method, which belongs to the `Object` superclass. The `runtimeType` property also comes from `Object` and gives the object type at runtime.

Can't Instantiate Abstract Classes

You can't create an object from an abstract class. See for yourself by writing the line below:

```
final animal = Animal();
```

You'll get the following error:

```
Abstract classes can't be instantiated.
Try creating an instance of a concrete subtype.
```

Isn't that good advice! That's what you're going to do next.

Concrete Subclass

Create a concrete `Platypus` now. Stop thinking about cement. Just add the following empty class to your IDE below your `Animal` class:

```
class Platypus extends Animal {}
```

Immediately you'll notice the wavy red line:

```
class Platypus extends Animal {}
```

That's not because you spelled platypus wrong. It really does have a *y*. Rather, the error is because when you extend an abstract class, you must provide an implementation of any abstract methods, which in this case are `eat` and `move`.

Adding the Missing Methods

You could write the methods yourself, but VS Code gives you a shortcut. Put your cursor on `Platypus` and press `Command+.` on a Mac or `Control+.` on a PC. You'll see the following pop-up:

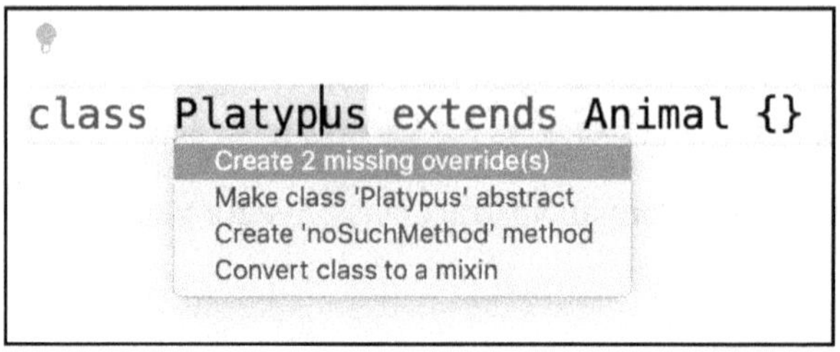

To quickly add the missing methods, choose **Create 2 missing override(s)**.

This will give you the following code:

```
class Platypus extends Animal {
  @override
  void eat() {
    // TODO: implement eat
  }

  @override
  void move() {
    // TODO: implement move
  }
}
```

Starting a comment with `TODO:` is a common way to mark parts of your code where you need to do more work. Later, you can search your entire project in VS Code for the remaining TODOs by pressing **Command+Shift+F** on a Mac or **Control+Shift+F** on a PC and writing "TODO" in the search box. You're going to complete these TODOs right now, though.

Filling in the TODOs

Since this is a concrete class, it needs to provide the actual implementation of the `eat` and `move` methods. In the `eat` method body, add the following line:

```
print('Munch munch');
```

A platypus may not have teeth, but it should still be able to munch.

In the move method, add:

```
print('Glide glide');
```

As was true with subclassing normal classes, abstract class subclasses can also have their own unique methods. Add the following method to Platypus:

```
void layEggs() {
  print('Plop plop');
}
```

Readers who are well-acquainted with how platypuses (Or is it platypi?) eat, swim and give birth can make additional word suggestions for the next edition of this book.

Testing the Results

Test your code out now in main:

```
final platypus = Platypus();
print(platypus.isAlive);
platypus.eat();
platypus.move();
platypus.layEggs();
print(platypus);
```

Run the code to see the following:

```
true
Munch munch
Glide glide
Plop plop
I'm a Platypus
```

Look at what this tells you:

- A concrete class has access to concrete data, like isAlive, from its abstract parent class.
- Dart recognized that the runtime type was Platypus, even though runtimeType comes from Object and was accessed in the toString method of Animal.

Treating Concrete Classes as Abstract

There is one more interesting thing to do before moving on. In the line where you declared `platypus`, hover your cursor over the variable name:

```
            Platypus platypus
final platypus = Platypus();
```

Dart infers `platypus` to be of type `Platypus`. That's normal, but here's the interesting part. Replace that line with the following one, adding the `Animal` type annotation:

```
Animal platypus = Platypus();
```

Hover your cursor over `platypus` again:

```
            Animal platypus
Animal platypus = Platypus();
```

Now Dart sees `platypus` as merely an `Animal` with no more special ability to lay eggs. Comment out the line calling the `layEggs` method:

```
// platypus.layEggs();
```

Run the code again paying special attention to the `print(platypus)` results:

```
I'm a Platypus
```

At compile time, Dart treats `platypus` like an `Animal` even though at runtime Dart knows it's a `Platypus`. This is useful when you don't care about about the concrete implementation of an abstract class, but you only care that it's an `Animal` with `Animal` characteristics.

Now, you're probably thinking, "Making animal classes is very cute and all, but how does this help me save data on the awesome new social media app I'm making?" That's where interfaces come in. See you in the next chapter!

Challenges

Before moving on, here's a challenge to test your knowledge of abstract classes. It's best if you try to solve it yourself, but a solution is available with the supplementary materials for this book if you get stuck.

Challenge 1: Saving It Somewhere

1. Create an abstract class named `Storage` with `print` statements in the `save` and `retrieve` methods.

2. Extend `Storage` with concrete classes named `LocalStorage` and `CloudStorage`.

Key Points

- Abstract classes define class members and may or may not contain concrete logic.
- Abstract classes can't be instantiated.
- Concrete classes can extend abstract classes.

Chapter 5: Interfaces

By Jonathan Sande

Interfaces are similar to abstract classes in that they let you define the behavior you expect for all classes that implement the interface. They're a means of hiding the implementation details of the concrete classes from the rest of your code. Why is that important? To answer that question it's helpful to understand a little about architecture. Not the Taj Mahal kind of architecture, software architecture.

Software Architecture

When you're building an app, your goal should be to keep core business logic separate from infrastructure like the UI, database, network and third-party packages. Why? The core business logic doesn't change frequently, while the infrastructure often does. Mixing unstable code with stable would cause the stable code to become unstable.

> Note: **Business logic**, which is sometimes called **business rules** or **domain logic**, refers to the essence of what your app does. The business logic of a calculator app would be the mathematical calculations themselves. Those calculations don't depend on what your UI looks like or how you store the answers.

The following image shows an idealized app with the stable business logic in the middle and the more volatile infrastructure parts surrounding it:

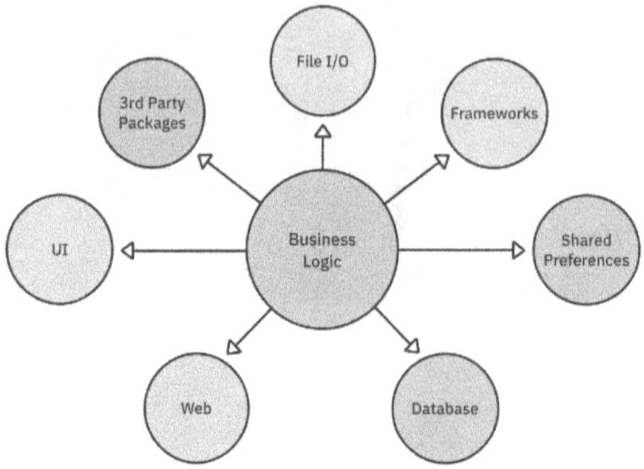

The UI shouldn't communicate directly with the web. You also shouldn't scatter direct calls to the database across your app. Everything goes through the central business logic. In addition to that, the business logic shouldn't know any implementation details about the infrastructure.

This gives you a plug-in-style architecture, where you can swap one database framework for another and the rest of the app won't even know anything changed. You could replace your mobile UI with a desktop UI, and the rest of the app wouldn't care. This is useful for building scalable, maintainable and testable apps.

Communication Rules

Here's where interfaces come in. An **interface** is a description of how communication will be managed between two parties. A phone number is a type of interface. If you want to call your friend, you have to dial your friend's phone number. Dialing a different number won't work. Another word for interface is **protocol**, as in Internet Protocol (IP) or Hypertext Transfer Protocol (HTTP). Those protocols are the rules for how communication happens among the users of the protocol.

When you create an interface in Dart, you define the rules for how one part of your codebase will communicate with another part. As long as both parts follow the interface rules, each part can change independently of the other. This makes your app much more manageable. In team settings, interfaces also allow different people to work on different parts of the codebase without worrying that they're going to mess up someone else's code.

Another related term you've probably heard before is **API**, or **Application Programming Interface**. An API is the public-facing set of methods that allow one program or code base to talk to another. Up to now, you've only been a consumer of other developers' APIs. For example, you've been using the API that came with the Dart SDK every time you write Dart code. Or if you've experimented with Flutter, you might have used the Firebase API or some other third-party API that you got from a Pub package. You've come to the point now, though, where you're ready to begin developing your own APIs.

Separating Business Logic From Infrastructure

In the image below, you can see the interface is between the business logic and the code for accessing the database.

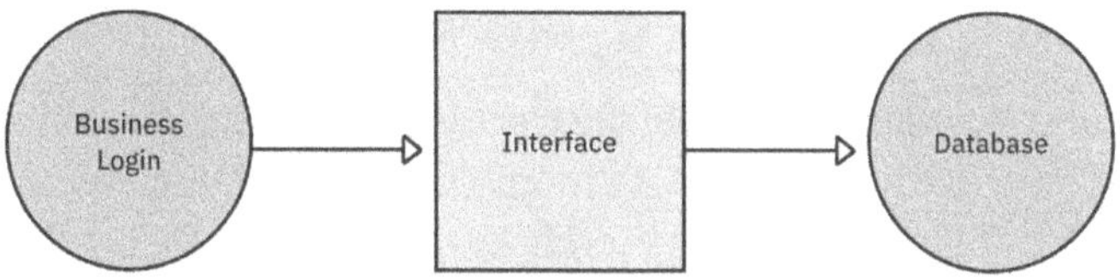

The business logic doesn't know anything about the database. It's just talking to the interface. That means you could even swap out the database for a completely different form of storage, like cloud storage or file storage. The business logic doesn't care.

There's a famous adage related to this that goes, **code against interfaces, not implementations**. You define an interface, and then you code your app to use that interface only. While you must implement the interface with concrete classes, the rest of your app shouldn't know anything about those concrete classes, only the interface.

Coding an Interface in Dart

There's no `interface` keyword in Dart. Instead, you can use any class as an interface. Since only the field and method names are important, most interfaces are made from abstract classes that contain no logic.

Creating an Abstract Interface Class

Say you want to make a weather app, and your business logic needs to get the current temperature in some city. Since those are the requirements, your Dart interface class would look like this:

```
abstract class DataRepository {
  double? fetchTemperature(String city);
}
```

Note that **repository** is a common term to call an interface that hides the details of how data is stored and retrieved. Also, the reason the result of `fetchTemperature` is nullable is that someone might ask for the temperature in a city that doesn't exist.

Implementing the Interface

The Dart class above was just a normal abstract class, like the one you made earlier. However, when creating a concrete class to implement the interface, you use the `implements` keyword instead of the `extends` keyword.

Add the following concrete class:

```
class FakeWebServer implements DataRepository {
  @override
  double? fetchTemperature(String city) {
    return 42.0;
  }
}
```

Here are a couple of points to note:

- Besides the benefits mentioned previously, another great advantage of using an interface is that you can create mock implementations to temporarily replace real implementations. In the `FakeWebServer` class, you're simply returning a random number instead of going to all the work of contacting a real server. This allows you to have a "working" app until you get around to writing the code to contact the web server. This is also useful when you're testing your code and you don't want to wait for a real connection to the server.

- Speaking of waiting for a web server, a real interface would return a type of `Future<double?>` instead of returning `double?` directly. However, you haven't read Chapter 12, "Futures", yet, so this example omits the `Future` part.

Using the Interface

How do you use the interface on the business logic side? Remember that you can't instantiate an abstract class, so this won't work:

```
final repository = DataRepository();
```

You could potentially use the `FakeWebServer` implementation directly like so:

```
final DataRepository repository = FakeWebServer();
final temperature = repository.fetchTemperature('Berlin');
```

But this defeats the whole point of trying to keep the implementation details separate from the business logic. When you get around to swapping out the `FakeWebServer` with another class, you'll have to go back and make updates at every place in your business logic that mentions it.

Adding a Factory Constructor

Do you remember learning about factory constructors *Dart Apprentice: Fundamentals*? If you do, you'll recall that factory constructors can return subclasses. Add the following line to your interface class:

```
factory DataRepository() => FakeWebServer();
```

Your interface should look like this now:

```
abstract class DataRepository {
  factory DataRepository() => FakeWebServer();
  double? fetchTemperature(String city);
}
```

Since `FakeWebServer` is a subclass of `DataRepository`, the factory constructor is allowed to return it. The neat trick is that by using an unnamed constructor for the factory, you can make it look like it's possible to instantiate the class now.

Write the following in `main`:

```
final repository = DataRepository();
final temperature = repository.fetchTemperature('Manila');
```

Ah, now your code on this side has no idea that that repository is actually `FakeWebServer`. When it comes time to swap in the real implementation, you only need to update the subclass returned by the factory constructor in the `DataRepository` interface.

> **Note**: In the code above, you used a factory to return the concrete implementation of the interface. There are other options, though. Do a search for **service locators** (of which the `get_it` package is a good example) and **dependency injection** to learn more about this topic.

Interfaces and the Dart SDK

If you browse the Dart source code, which you can do by Command or Control-clicking Dart class names like `int` or `List` or `String`, you'll see that Dart makes heavy use of interfaces to define its API. That allows the Dart team to change the implementation details without affecting developers. The only time developers are affected is when the interface changes.

This concept is key to the flexibility that Dart has as a language. The Dart VM implements the interface one way and gives you the ability to hot-reload your Flutter apps. The `dart compile js` tool implements the interface using JavaScript and gives you the ability to run your code on the web. The `dart compile exe` tool implements the interface on Windows or Linux or Mac to let you run your code on those platforms.

The implementation details are different for every platform, but you don't have to worry about that because your code will only talk to the interface, not to the platform. Are you starting to see how powerful interfaces can be?

Extending vs Implementing

There are a couple of differences between `extends` and `implements`. Dart only allows you to extend a single superclass. This is known as **single inheritance**, which is in contrast with other languages that allow **multiple inheritance**.

So the following is not allowed in Dart:

```
class MySubclass extends OneClass, AnotherClass {} // Not OK
```

However, you can implement more than one interface:

```
class MyClass implements OneClass, AnotherClass {} // OK
```

You can also combine `extends` and `implements`:

```
class MySubclass extends OneClass implements AnotherClass {}
```

But what's the difference between just extending or implementing? That is, how are these two lines different:

```
class SomeClass extends AnotherClass {}
class SomeClass implements AnotherClass {}
```

When you extend `AnotherClass`, `SomeClass` has access to any logic or variables in `AnotherClass`. However, if `SomeClass` *implements* `AnotherClass`, `SomeClass` must provide its own version of all methods and variables in `AnotherClass`.

Example of Extending

Assume `AnotherClass` looks like the following:

```
class AnotherClass {
  int myField = 42;
  void myMethod() => print(myField);
}
```

You can extend it like this with no issue:

```
class SomeClass extends AnotherClass {}
```

Check that `SomeClass` objects have access to `AnotherClass` data and methods:

```
final someClass = SomeClass();
print(someClass.myField);      // 42
someClass.myMethod();          // 42
```

Run that and you'll see 42 printed twice.

Example of Implementing

Using `implements` in the same way doesn't work:

```
class SomeClass implements AnotherClass {} // Not OK
```

The `implements` keyword tells Dart that you only want the field types and method signatures. You'll provide the concrete implementation details for everything yourself. How you implement it is up to you, as demonstrated in the following example:

```
class SomeClass implements AnotherClass {
  @override
  int myField = 0;

  @override
  void myMethod() => print('Hello');
}
```

Test that code again as before:

```
final someClass = SomeClass();
print(someClass.myField);      // 0
someClass.myMethod();          // Hello
```

This time you see your custom implementation results in `0` and `Hello`.

Challenges

Before moving on, here are some challenges to test your knowledge of interfaces. It's best if you try to solve them yourself, but solutions are available with the supplementary materials for this book if you get stuck.

Challenge 1: Fizzy Bottles

1. Create an interface called `Bottle` and add a method to it called `open`.
2. Create a concrete class called `SodaBottle` that implements `Bottle` and prints "Fizz fizz" when `open` is called.
3. Add a factory constructor to `Bottle` that returns a `SodaBottle` instance.
4. Instantiate `SodaBottle` by using the `Bottle` factory constructor and call `open` on the object.

Challenge 2: Fake Notes

Design an interface to sit between the business logic of your note-taking app and a SQL database. After that, implement a fake database class that will return mock data.

Key Points

- One rule of clean architecture is to separate business logic from infrastructure logic like the UI, storage, third-party packages and the network.
- Interfaces define a protocol for code communication.
- Use the `implements` keyword to create an interface.
- Dart only allows single inheritance on its classes.

Where to Go From Here?

Once you learn how to use a hammer, everything will look like a nail. Now that you know about abstract classes and interfaces, you might be tempted to use them all the time. Don't over-engineer your apps, though. Start simple, and add abstraction as you need it.

Throughout the *Dart Apprentice* books, you've gotten a few ideas for writing clean code. However, the principles of building clean architecture take clean coding to a whole new level. You won't master the skill all at once, but reading books and articles and watching videos on the subject will help you grow as a software engineer.

Chapter 6: Mixins

By Jonathan Sande

Mixins are an interesting feature of Dart that you might not be familiar with, even if you know other programming languages. They're a way to reuse methods or variables among otherwise unrelated classes.

> **Note**: For you Swift developers, Dart mixins work like protocol extensions.

Before showing you what mixins look like, you'll first take a look at why you need them.

Problems With Extending and Implementing

Think back to the `Animal` examples again. Say you've got a bunch of birds, so you're carefully planning an abstract class to represent them. Here's what you come up with:

```
abstract class Bird {
  void fly();
  void layEggs();
}
```

"It's looking good!" you think. "I'm getting the hang of this." So you try it out on `Robin`:

```
class Robin extends Bird {
  @override
  void fly() {
    print('Swoosh swoosh');
  }

  @override
  void layEggs() {
    print('Plop plop');
  }
}
```

"Perfect!" You smile contentedly at your handiwork.

Then you hear a sound behind you.

"Munch, munch. Glide, glide. Plop, plop. I'm a platypus."

Oh. Right. The platypus.

Here's the code you wrote for `Platypus` back in Chapter 3, "Inheritance":

```
abstract class Animal {
  bool isAlive = true;
  void eat();
  void move();

  @override
  String toString() {
    return "I'm a $runtimeType";
  }
}
```

```
class Platypus extends Animal {
  @override
  void eat() {
    print('Munch munch');
  }

  @override
  void move() {
    print('Glide glide');
  }

  void layEggs() {
    print('Plop plop');
  }
}
```

Your `layEggs` code for `Robin` is exactly the same as it is for `Platypus`. That means you're duplicating code, which violates the DRY principle. If there are any future changes to `layEggs`, you'll have to remember to change both instances. Consider your options:

1. Platypus can't extend `Bird` or `Robin`, because platypi can't fly.
2. Birds probably shouldn't extend `Platypus`, because who knows when you're going to add the `stingWithVenomSpur` method?
3. You could create an `EggLayer` class and have `Bird` and `Platypus` both extend that. But then what about flying? Make a `Flyer` class, too? Dart only allows you to extend one class, so that won't work.
4. You could have birds implement `EggLayer` and `Flyer` while Platypus implements only `EggLayer`. But then you're back to code duplication since implementing requires you to supply the implementation code for every class.

The solution? Mixins!

Mixing in Code

To make a **mixin**, you take whatever concrete code you want to share with different classes, and package it in its own special mixin class.

Write the following two mixins:

```
mixin EggLayer {
  void layEggs() {
    print('Plop plop');
  }
}

mixin Flyer {
  void fly() {
    print('Swoosh swoosh');
  }
}
```

The `mixin` keyword indicates that these classes can *only* be used as mixins. You can also use a normal class as a mixin as long as that class doesn't extend another non-`Object` class. So if you wanted to use `EggLayer` as a normal class, then just replace the `mixin` keyword with `class` or `abstract class`.

Now refactor `Robin` as follows, using the `with` keyword to identify the mixins:

```
class Robin extends Bird with EggLayer, Flyer {}
```

There are two mixins, so you separate them with a comma. Since those two mixins contain all the code that `Bird` needs, the class body is now empty.

Refactor `Platypus` as well:

```
class Platypus extends Animal with EggLayer {
  @override
  void eat() {
    print('Munch munch');
  }

  @override
  void move() {
    print('Glide glide');
  }
}
```

The `layEggs` logic has moved to the mixin. Now both `Robin` and `Platypus` share the code that the `EggLayer` mixin contains. Just to make sure it works, run the following code:

```
final platypus = Platypus();
final robin = Robin();
platypus.layEggs();
robin.layEggs();
```

Four plops, and all is well.

Challenges

Before moving on, here are some challenges to test your knowledge of mixins. It's best if you try to solve them yourself, but solutions are available with the supplementary materials for this book if you get stuck.

Challenge 1: Calculator

1. Create a class called `Calculator` with a method called `sum` that prints the sum of any two integers you give it.

2. Extract the logic in `sum` to a mixin called `Adder`.

3. Use the mixin in `Calculator`.

Challenge 2: Heavy Monotremes

Dart has a class named `Comparable`, which is used by the `sort` method of `List` to sort its elements.

1. Add a `weight` field to the `Platypus` class you made earlier.

2. Then make `Platypus` implement `Comparable` so that when you have a list of `Platypus` objects, calling `sort` on the list will sort them by weight.

Key Points

- Mixins allow you to share code between classes.
- You can use any class as a mixin as long as it doesn't extend anything besides `Object`.
- Using the `mixin` keyword means that a class can *only* be used as a mixin.

Chapter 7: Extension Methods

By Jonathan Sande

Up to this point in the book, you've been writing your own classes and methods. Often, though, you use other people's classes when you're programming. Those classes may be part of a core Dart library, or they may be from packages on Pub. In either case, you don't have the ability to modify them at will.

However, Dart has a feature called **extension methods** that allows you to add functionality to existing classes. Even though they're called extension *methods*, you can also add other members like getters, setters or even operators.

Extension Syntax

To make an extension, you use the following syntax:

```
extension on SomeClass {
  // your custom code
}
```

This should be located at the top level in a file, that is, not inside another class or function. Replace `SomeClass` with whatever class you want to add extra functionality to.

You may give the extension itself a name if you like. In that case, the syntax is as follows:

```
extension YourExtensionName on SomeClass {
  // your custom code
}
```

You can use whatever name you like in place of `YourExtensionName`. The name is only used to show or hide the extension when importing it in another library.

Have a look at a few of the following examples to see how extension methods work.

String Extension Example

Did you ever make secret codes when you were a kid, like `a=1`, `b=2`, `c=3`, and so on? For this example, you're going to make an extension that will convert a string into a secret coded message. Then you'll add another extension method to decode it.

In this secret code, each letter will be bumped up to the next one. So **a** will be **b**, **b** will be **c**, and so on. To accomplish that, you'll increase the Unicode value of each code point in the input string by `1`. If the original message were "abc", the encoded message should be "bcd".

Solving in the Normal Way

First, solve the problem as you would with a normal function. Add the following to your project:

```
String encode(String input) {
  final output = StringBuffer();
  for (final codePoint in input.runes) {
    output.writeCharCode(codePoint + 1);
  }
  return output.toString();
}
```

You loop through each Unicode code point and increment it by 1 before writing it to `output`. Finally, you convert the `StringBuffer` back to a regular `String` and return it.

Test your code out by writing the code below in `main`:

```
final original = 'abc';
final secret = encode(original);
print(secret);
```

Run that and you'll see the result is `bcd`. It works!

Converting to an Extension

The next step is to convert the `encode` function above to an extension so that you can use it like so:

```
final secret = 'abc'.encoded;
```

Since this extension won't mutate the original string itself, a naming convention is to use an adjective rather than a commanding verb. That's the reason for choosing `encoded`, rather than `encode`, for the extension name.

Like classes, extensions can't be located inside of a function. So add the following code somewhere outside of `main`:

```
extension on String {
  String get encoded {
    final output = StringBuffer();
    for (final codePoint in runes) {
      output.writeCharCode(codePoint + 1);
    }
    return output.toString();
```

```
  }
}
```

Look at what's changed here from its previous form as a function:

- The keywords `extension on` are what make this an extension. You can add whatever you want inside the body. It's as if `String` were your own class now.
- Rather than making a normal method, you can use a getter method. This makes it so that you can call the extension using `encoded`, without the parentheses, rather than `encoded()`.
- Since you're inside `String` already, there's no need to pass `input` as an argument. If you need a reference to the string object, you can use the `this` keyword. Thus, instead of `input.runes`, you could write `this.runes`. However, `this` is unnecessary and you can directly access `runes`. Remember that `runes` is a member of `String` and you're inside `String`.

Check that the extension works:

```
final secret = 'abc'.encoded;
print(secret);
```

You should see `bcd` as the output. Nice! It still works.

Adding a Decode Extension

Add the `decoded` method inside the body of the `String` extension as well:

```
String get decoded {
  final output = StringBuffer();
  for (final codePoint in runes) {
    output.writeCharCode(codePoint - 1);
  }
  return output.toString();
}
```

If you compare this to the `encoded` method, though, there's a lot of code duplication. Whenever you see code duplication, you should think about how to make it DRY.

Refactoring to Remove Code Duplication

Refactor your String extension by replacing the entire extension with the following:

```
extension on String {
  String get encoded => _code(1);
  String get decoded => _code(-1);

  String _code(int step) {
    final output = StringBuffer();
    for (final codePoint in runes) {
      output.writeCharCode(codePoint + step);
    }
    return output.toString();
  }
}
```

Now the private _code method factors out all of the common parts of encoded and decoded. That's better.

Testing the Results

To make sure that everything works, test both methods like so:

```
final original = 'I like extensions!';
final secret = original.encoded;
final revealed = secret.decoded;
print(secret);
print(revealed);
```

This will display the following encoded and decoded messages:

```
J!mjlf!fyufotjpot"
I like extensions!
```

Great! Now you can amuse your friends by giving them encoded messages. They're actually a lot of fun to solve.

Int Extension Example

Here's an example of an extension on `int`.

```
extension on int {
  int get cubed {
    return this * this * this;
  }
}
```

Notice the use of `this` to get a reference to the `int` object, which will be 5 in the example below.

You use the extension like so:

```
print(5.cubed);
```

The answer is 125.

As you can see, you can do a lot with extensions. Although they can be very powerful, extensions by definition add non-standard behavior, and this can make it harder for other developers to understand your code. Use extensions when they make sense, but try not to overuse them.

Oh, one more thing.

```
Uif!tfdsfu!up!mfbsojoh!Ebsu!xfmm!jt!up!
dg"ewtkqwu"cpf"lwuv"vt{"vjkpiu0"Vlqfh#|rx*uh#uhdglqj#wklv/
#wkdw#reylrxvo|#ghvfulehv#|rx1#Kssh$nsf%
```

Challenges

Before moving on, here's a challenge to test your knowledge of extension methods. It's best if you try to solve it yourself, but a solution is available with the supplementary materials for this book if you get stuck.

Challenge 1: Time to Code

Dart has a `Duration` class for expressing lengths of time. Make an extension on `int` so that you can express a duration like so:

```
final timeRemaining = 3.minutes;
```

Key Points

- Extension methods allow you to give additional functionality to classes that are not your own.
- Use extensions when they make sense, but try not to overuse them.

Chapter 8: Generics

By Jonathan Sande

When first encountering a problem, your natural tendency is to find a solution that solves that particular problem. You don't worry about related problems; you care only about the problem that's troubling you now.

Say you want to learn French. You might begin by trying to memorize sentences from a phrasebook. That turns out to be a slow and ineffective method. After trying several other language-learning techniques, you discover that lots of easy listening and reading input helps you learn much faster. Your problem is solved; you've learned French well enough to understand and communicate.

Then, you decide to learn Chinese. Do you return to the phrasebooks? Of course not. There's no need to learn how to learn all over again. You already found a language-learning method that worked for you with French. You can use that same method with Chinese. You might need to pick up a few more techniques to help you learn those characters, but the overall method remains the same: lots of easy listening and reading input.

The more languages you learn, the better you get at learning languages. You've generalized the language learning process to the point where you know exactly how you would tackle any language.

Instead of French, Chinese or Urdu, now think `String`, `bool` and `int`. In Dart, **generics** refers to generalizing specific types so you can handle them all similarly. This chapter will teach not only how to *use* generic types but also how to *create* new generic classes and collections.

Using Generics

You've already encountered Dart generics earlier if you read *Dart Apprentice: Fundamentals*. In Chapter 12, "Lists", you saw this example:

```
List<String> snacks = [];
```

Whenever you see the < > angle brackets surrounding a type, you should think, "Hey, that's generics!" `List` is a generic collection. It can hold strings, integers, doubles or any other type. By specifying `<String>` in angle brackets, you're declaring this list will hold only strings.

Replace the line above with a fuller example:

```
List<String> snacks = ['chips', 'nuts'];
```

Each element in the list is a string: `'chips'` is a string and so is `'nuts'`. If you tried to add the integer `42`, Dart would complain at you.

See for yourself. Replace the line above with the following:

```
List<String> snacks = ['chips', 'nuts', 42];
```

The compiler gives the following error message:

```
The element type 'int' can't be assigned to the list type
'String'.
```

No integers are allowed in a string list! If you want to allow both integers and strings in the same list, you can set the list type to `Object`, which is a supertype of both `String` and `int`. Replace `String` in the line above with `Object`:

```
List<Object> snacks = ['chips', 'nuts', 42];
```

Now, the compiler no longer complains.

Because `List` is generic, it can contain any type. Here are some more examples:

```
List<int> integerList = [3, 1, 4];
List<double> doubleList = [3.14, 8.0, 0.001];
List<bool> booleanList = [true, false, false];
```

These are all generics at work. A single type `List` can store an ordered collection of any other type. There was no need to create different classes like `IntList`, `DoubleList` or `BoolList` for each type. If the language had been designed like that, it would have been like reinventing the wheel every time you needed a new list for a different type. Generics prevents code duplication.

All Dart collections use generics, not just `List`. For example, `Set` and `Map` do as well:

```
Set<int> integerSet = {3, 1, 4};
Map<int, String> intToStringMap = {1: 'one', 2: 'two', 3:
'three'};
```

`Map` uses generic types for both the key and the value. This means you can map `int` to `String`, or `String` to `int`, or `bool` to `double` and so on.

Using generic classes is easy enough. Now, you'll take your skills to the next level by learning to *create* generic classes and functions.

Creating Generic Classes

Collections are where you see generics the most, so to give you something to practice on, you're going to create a generic collection called a tree. Trees are an important data structure you'll find in many computer science applications. Some examples include:

- Binary trees.
- Binary search trees.
- Priority Queues.
- Flutter UI widget trees.

A **binary tree** is one of the simplest types of trees. It consists of nodes, where each node can have up to two children. The image below illustrates this:

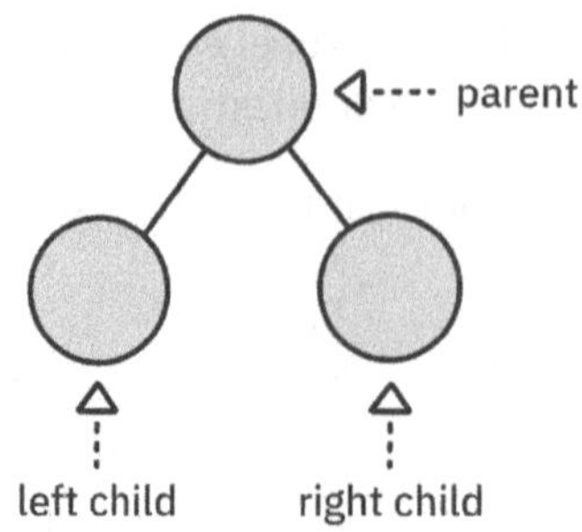

A node with children is called a **parent**, and the children are differentiated by calling them the **left child** and the **right child**.

In addition to having children, nodes also store a value. A tree that holds integers might look like so:

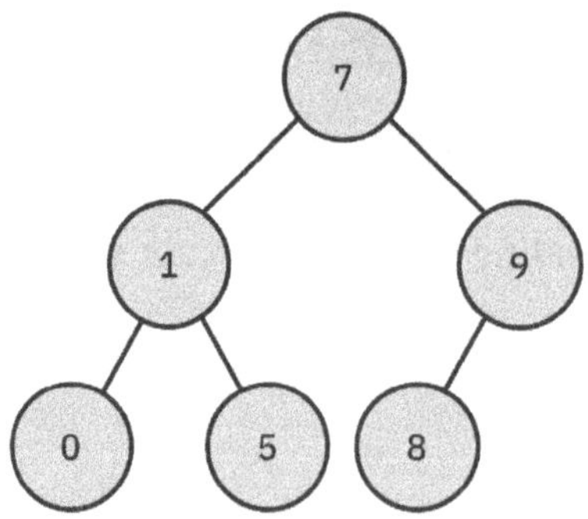

The top node of the tree is called the **root node**. Whoever put the root at the top of the tree was probably standing on their head that day.

The values in this particular tree are integers, but you could store any data type there.

Starting With a Non-Generic Integer Class

You'll begin by creating a node and a tree in a non-generic way. Then, you'll generalize your approach so it can handle any data type.

Create the following class below the `main` method in your Dart project:

```
class IntNode {
  IntNode(this.value);
  int value;

  IntNode? leftChild;
  IntNode? rightChild;
}
```

`IntNode` has three properties. The constructor allows you to set the node's `value`. `leftChild` and `rightChild` are optional because not every node has children.

Now, create the tree you saw in the diagram above by adding the following function below `main`:

```
IntNode createIntTree() {
  final zero = IntNode(0);
  final one = IntNode(1);
  final five = IntNode(5);
  final seven = IntNode(7);
  final eight = IntNode(8);
  final nine = IntNode(9);

  seven.leftChild = one;
  one.leftChild = zero;
  one.rightChild = five;
  seven.rightChild = nine;
  nine.leftChild = eight;

  return seven;
}
```

You return `seven` because it's the root node and contains the links to the other nodes in the tree. Returning any other node would only provide a portion of the tree. Parents link to their children, not the other way around.

Now, in `main`, create the tree by calling your function:

```
final intTree = createIntTree();
```

Reimplementing the Tree With String Nodes

You've built an integer tree. What would you need to change if you wanted to put strings in the tree like so:

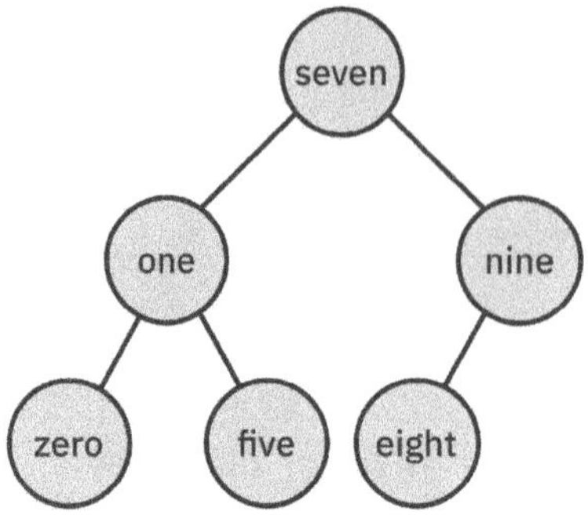

For that, you would need to change the node's data type. However, you can't change the data type of `value` in `IntTree` without messing up the integer tree you made earlier. So create a new class like the one below:

```
class StringNode {
  StringNode(this.value);
  String value;

  StringNode? leftChild;
  StringNode? rightChild;
}
```

Now, `value` is of type `String` instead of `int`.

Next, add a function below `main` to create the tree of strings that you saw in the diagram above:

```
StringNode createStringTree() {
  final zero = StringNode('zero');
  final one = StringNode('one');
  final five = StringNode('five');
  final seven = StringNode('seven');
  final eight = StringNode('eight');
  final nine = StringNode('nine');

  seven.leftChild = one;
  one.leftChild = zero;
  one.rightChild = five;
  seven.rightChild = nine;
  nine.leftChild = eight;
```

```
  return seven;
}
```

The logic is all the same as the `IntNode` tree you made earlier.

Create the tree in `main` like so:

```
final stringTree = createStringTree();
```

Comparing the Duplication

Currently, you've got a lot of code duplication. Here's the integer node class again:

```
class IntNode {
  IntNode(this.value);
  int value;

  IntNode? leftChild;
  IntNode? rightChild;
}
```

And here's the string node class:

```
class StringNode {
  StringNode(this.value);
  String value;

  StringNode? leftChild;
  StringNode? rightChild;
}
```

And what if you wanted to make a tree of Boolean values? Here's what the node class would look like:

```
class BooleanNode {
  BooleanNode(this.value);
  bool value;

  BooleanNode? leftChild;
  BooleanNode? rightChild;
}
```

And then, if you decided you needed a tree of floating-point values, you'd have to create a whole new class:

```
class DoubleNode {
  DoubleNode(this.value);
  double value;

  DoubleNode? leftChild;
  DoubleNode? rightChild;
}
```

And on it goes for every new data type you want to use. You must create a new class to hold the new type, duplicating lots of code each time.

Creating a Generic Node

Using generics allows you to remove all the duplication you saw in the previous section.

Add the following class to your project:

```
class Node<T> {
  Node(this.value);
  T value;

  Node<T>? leftChild;
  Node<T>? rightChild;
}
```

This time, the angle brackets show that this is a class with a generic type. The `T` here represents any *type*. You don't have to use the letter T, but it's customary to use single capital letters when specifying a generic type.

Updating the Integer Tree

Now, replace `createIntTree` with the updated version that uses generics:

```
Node<int> createIntTree() {
  final zero = Node(0);
  final one = Node(1);
  final five = Node(5);
  final seven = Node(7);
  final eight = Node(8);
  final nine = Node(9);

  seven.leftChild = one;
  one.leftChild = zero;
```

```
  one.rightChild = five;
  seven.rightChild = nine;
  nine.leftChild = eight;

  return seven;
}
```

This time, the return type is `Node<int>` instead of `IntNode`. You specify `int` inside the angle brackets so users of `createIntTree` know the values inside the tree are integers. Hover your cursor over `zero`, and you'll see that Dart already infers the type to be `Node<int>` because it knows `0` is an integer.

Back in `main`, the code is still the same:

```
final intTree = createIntTree();
```

Hover your cursor over `intTree`, and you'll see that the inferred type is `Node<int>`. Dart knows it because you wrote that as the return type of `createIntTree`.

Updating the String Tree

Update `createStringTree` in the same way. Replace the previous function with the following version:

```
Node<String> createStringTree() {
  final zero = Node('zero');
  final one = Node('one');
  final five = Node('five');
  final seven = Node('seven');
  final eight = Node('eight');
  final nine = Node('nine');

  seven.leftChild = one;
  one.leftChild = zero;
  one.rightChild = five;
  seven.rightChild = nine;
  nine.leftChild = eight;

  return seven;
}
```

The function return type is `Node<String>` this time instead of `StringNode`. Check that your generic `Node` class works by hovering your cursor over `zero`. You'll see the inferred type is also `Node<String>` because `'zero'` is a `String`. Your generic `Node` class works!

Creating Generic Functions

You've successfully made a generic `Node` class. However, the functions you wrote to build your tree aren't generic. `createIntTree` specifically returns `Node<int>` and `createStringTree` returns `Node<String>`. Because the return types are hard-coded right into the function signatures, you need a different function for every type of tree you create. This, too, is a lot of code duplication.

Generics are here to save the day because, in addition to generic classes, you can also make generic functions.

Storing a Tree in a List

Before giving you the code for the generic function, this is how it's going to work:

```
final tree = createTree([7, 1, 9, 0, 5, 8]);
```

`createTree` will take a list of some data type, be it `int`, `String` or whatever. Then the function will convert the list to a binary tree. It's possible to do that if you assume the first element in the list is the root-node value, the second element is the left-child value, the third element is the right-child value and so on, where the values in the list correspond to levels in the tree. The image below shows the list values and indexes laid out in a binary tree:

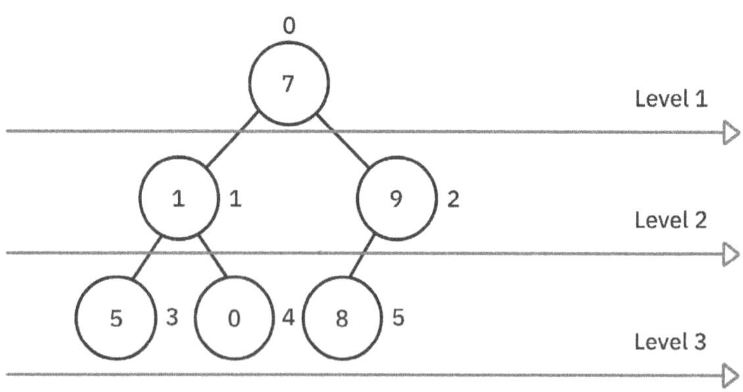

> **Note**: This data structure where a list stores the values of a tree is known as a **heap**. Read Chapter 13, "Heaps", in *Data Structures & Algorithms in Dart* to learn more.

Implementing the Function

Now that you've got a little background, add the following function below `main`:

```
// 1
Node<E>? createTree<E>(List<E> nodes, [int index = 0]) {
  // 2
  if (index >= nodes.length) return null;
  // 3
  final node = Node(nodes[index]);
  // 4
  final leftChildIndex = 2 * index + 1;
  final rightChildIndex = 2 * index + 2;
  // 5
  node.leftChild = createTree(nodes, leftChildIndex);
  node.rightChild = createTree(nodes, rightChildIndex);
  // 6
  return node;
}
```

Here are some notes corresponding to the numbered comments above:

1. This time, the letter you're using for the generic type is `E` instead of `T`. You could use `T` again, but it's customary to use `E` when creating a collection, which is a tree of nodes in this case. The `E` stands for *elements*.

2. When working with trees, recursive functions are very useful. A **recursive function** is a function that calls itself. If a function always calls itself, though, it could go on forever. Thus, it needs a way to stop calling itself. That's known as the **base case**. The base case for this recursive function is when the list index is out of range.

3. Take the value in the list at the given index and convert it to a new node. The default value of `index` is `0`, which is the root node.

4. In a binary tree where the values are laid out in a list by level, you can calculate the index of the left child by multiplying 2 times the parent index plus 1. The right child index is one beyond that.

5. Here's the recursive part. The function calls itself to create the child nodes. You pass in the indexes where the child values should be. If those indexes are out of range for the list, the base case will stop the recursion.

6. At the end of each recursion, `node` is the parent of some branch in the tree. And when all the recursions are finished, `node` is the root node.

Did that make your brain hurt? No worries. Recursion does that to everybody. The point of this chapter is to understand generics, not recursion. However, if you're interested, the best way to wrap your mind around recursion is to step through the code line by line and track what the computer is doing. You can do that with a paper and pencil. Or in Chapter 10, "Error Handling", you'll learn how to use the debugger in VS Code to pause execution and step through the code one line at a time. Feel free to jump ahead and learn how to do that now.

> **Note**: In addition to using `T` to represent a single generic *type* and `E` to represent generic *elements* in a collection, there are a few other letters developers use by convention. For a generic map, as in `Map<K, V>`, use `K` and `V` for the *keys* and *values*. Sometimes people use `R` for a function's *return* type. You can use other letters like `S` and `U` if you're already using `T` in the same generic function or class, though this is relatively rare.

Testing It Out

In `main`, write the following line:

```
final tree = createTree([7, 1, 9, 0, 5, 8]);
```

You could write another recursive function to print the contents of the tree, but for now, just print the values manually. Add the following code to `main`, below what you wrote previously:

```
print(tree?.value);
print(tree?.leftChild?.value);
print(tree?.rightChild?.value);
print(tree?.leftChild?.leftChild?.value);
print(tree?.leftChild?.rightChild?.value);
print(tree?.rightChild?.leftChild?.value);
print(tree?.rightChild?.rightChild?.value);
```

Because the nodes of a tree could be null, you have to access the children with the `?.` operator.

Run the code, and you'll see the result below:

```
7
1
9
0
5
8
null
```

This matches the layered order of your input list.

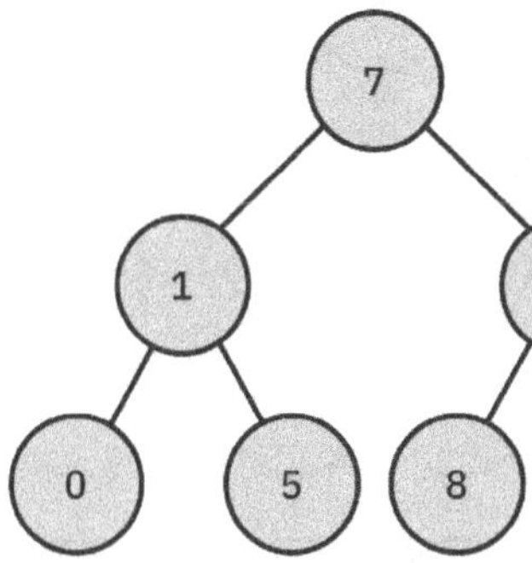

`createTree` is generic, so you should be able to change the data type of the elements and still have the function work. Replace the `createTree([7, 1, 9, 0, 5, 8])` line above with the following string version:

```
final tree = createTree(['seven', 'one', 'nine', 'zero', 'five',
'eight']);
```

The numbers are the same, but this time you're using strings.

Run the code again, and you'll see the following:

```
seven
one
nine
zero
five
eight
null
```

Generics of a Specified Subtype

In the example above, your `Node` could hold data of any type. Sometimes, though, you don't want to allow just any type. The values have to adhere to certain characteristics. A Binary Search Tree (BST) is an example of such a situation.

In a BST, the left child must always be less than the value of its parent, while the right child is always greater than or equal to the parent. Here's an example:

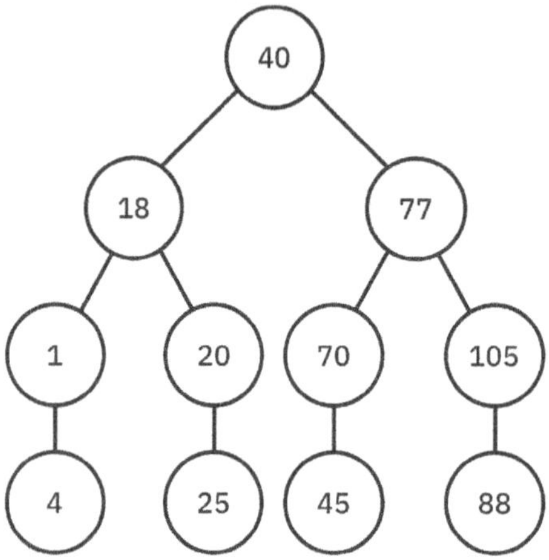

18 is less than 40, so it goes on the left, whereas 77 is greater, so it goes on the right. Likewise, the children of 18 and 77 follow the same pattern.

BST has applications in fast lookup. Here's how you would search for the value 105 in a list:

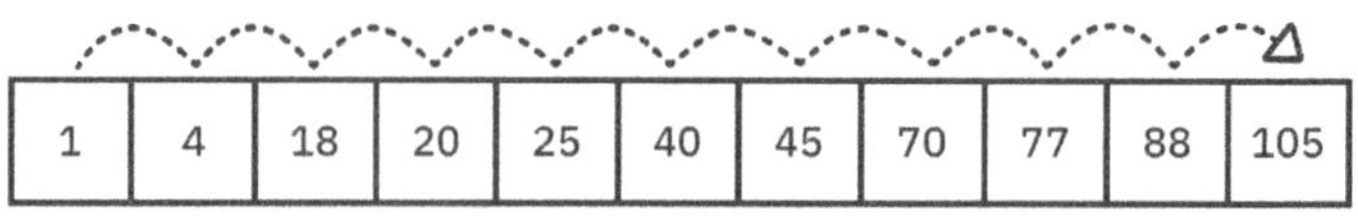

That took eleven steps.

Here's how you would search for 105 in a BST:

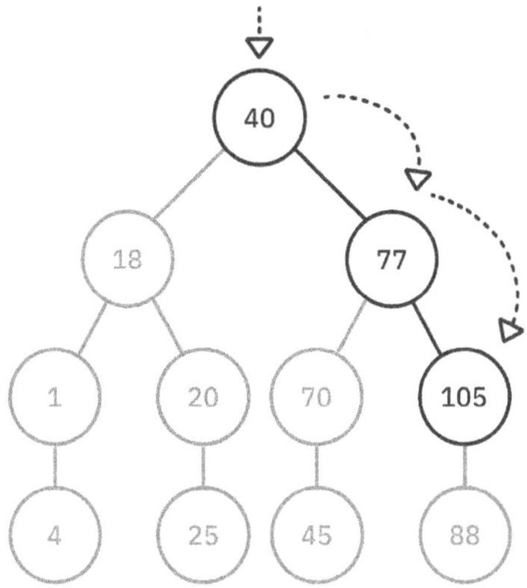

That's three steps instead of eleven. Much faster!

Implementing a Binary Search Tree

For BST to work, the types inside the nodes need to be comparable. It wouldn't make sense to create a BST of `User` objects or `Widget` objects because these objects aren't inherently comparable. That means you need a way of restricting the element type within the BST nodes.

The solution is to use the `extends` keyword. By only allowing data types that extend `Comparable`, you can guarantee the values in all the nodes will be comparable.

Create the following class:

```
class BinarySearchTree<E extends Comparable<E>> {
  Node<E>? root;
}
```

Here are a few explanatory points:

- `E` represents the type of the elements in the tree.
- The `extends` keyword goes inside the angle brackets to restrict the types that `E` can be. Only types that extend `Comparable` are allowed.
- You'll use the same `Node` class that you created earlier.

Now, add the following methods to `BinarySearchTree`:

```
void insert(E value) {
  root = _insertAt(root, value);
}

Node<E> _insertAt(Node<E>? node, E value) {
  // 1
  if (node == null) {
    return Node(value);
  }
  // 2
  if (value.compareTo(node.value) < 0) {
    node.leftChild = _insertAt(node.leftChild, value);
  } else {
    node.rightChild = _insertAt(node.rightChild, value);
  }
  // 3
  return node;
}
```

`_insertAt` is also a recursive function:

1. This is the base case. Create a new node if the parent node doesn't have a child at this location.
2. `compareTo` is a method on types that extend `Comparable`. This method returns `-1` if the first value is less than the second, `+1` if it's greater, and `0` if they're the same. If the value is smaller, insert the node at the left child. Otherwise, insert it at the right child. Calling `_insertAt` recursively searches the tree until it finds an empty child.
3. When the recursion finishes, this function will return the root node.

Building the Tree

For the example below, you'll create the following binary search tree:

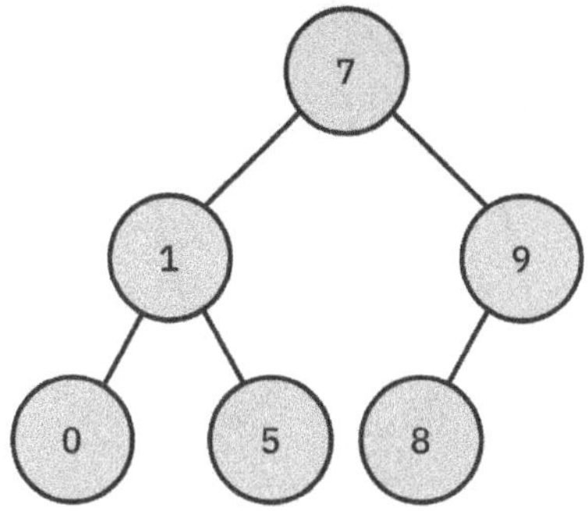

Add the code below to `main`:

```
var tree = BinarySearchTree<num>();
tree.insert(7);
tree.insert(1);
tree.insert(9);
tree.insert(0);
tree.insert(5);
tree.insert(8);
```

You specified the type as `num` rather than `int` because `int` doesn't directly implement `Comparable`, whereas `num` does.

To make printing easier, find your `Node` class and add the following override:

```
@override
String toString() {
  final left = leftChild?.toString() ?? '';
  final parent = value.toString();
  final right = rightChild?.toString() ?? '';
  return '$left $parent $right';
}
```

This recursively calls the `toString` methods of the left and right children. Because the parent value is calculated after the left child and before the right child, this is known as **in-order traversal**.

For a BST, this has the effect of printing the values in order from least to greatest:

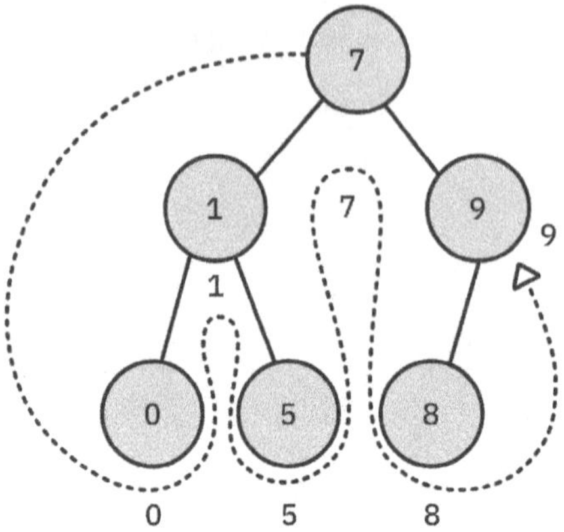

Find `BinarySearchTree` and add the following override:

```
@override
String toString() => root.toString();
```

`root` is the root node of the tree, so calling `root.toString` provides a string representation of all the values in the tree, starting at the left-most node and ending with the right-most one.

Add the following line to `main` and run the code:

```
print(tree);
```

You should see the following output in the console:

```
0 1 5 7 8 9
```

Your BST implementation works with integers. Because of generics, you wouldn't have any problem with doubles, either. Even strings would work because `String` is also comparable. The `insert` method when used with strings, though, would determine "greater than" and "less than" according to alphabetical order.

This completes the chapter. Having a handle on generics gives you a lot of flexibility in your coding.

Challenges

Before moving on, here are some challenges to test your knowledge of generics. It's best if you try to solve them yourself, but solutions are available with the supplementary materials for this book if you get stuck.

Challenge 1: A Stack of Numbers

A **stack** is a first-in-last-out (FILO) data structure. When you add new values, you put them on top of the stack, covering up the old values. Likewise, when you remove values from the stack, you can only remove them from the top of the stack.

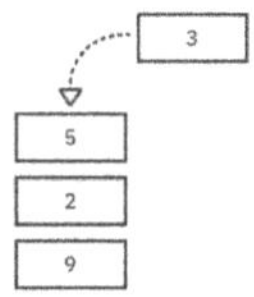

Create a class named `IntStack` with the following methods:

- `push`: adds an integer to the top of the stack.
- `pop`: removes and returns the top integer from the stack.
- `peek`: tells the value of the top integer in the stack without removing it.
- `isEmpty`: tells whether the stack is empty or not.
- `toString`: returns a string representation of the stack.

Use a `List` as the internal data structure.

Challenge 2: A Stack of Anything

Generalize your solution in Challenge 1 by creating a `Stack` class that can hold data of any type.

Key Points

- Generics allow classes and functions to accept data of any type.
- The angle brackets surrounding a type tell the class or function the data type it will use.
- Use the letter `T` as a generic symbol for any single type.
- Use the letter `E` to refer to the element type in a generic collection.
- You can restrict the range of allowable types by using the `extends` keyword within the angle brackets.

Where to Go From Here?

This chapter briefly referred to many topics covered in depth in the book Data Structures & Algorithms in Dart (https://www.kodeco.com/books/data-structures-algorithms-in-dart). Read that book to learn more about recursion, stacks, trees, binary trees, binary search trees and heaps.

Chapter 9: Enhanced Enums

By Jonathan Sande

Back in *Dart Apprentice: Fundamentals*, you learned about basic enums. They're a way to give names to a fixed number of options. An example would be the days of the week. Under the hood, each day has an index: `monday` is `0`, `tuesday` is `1` and so on through `sunday` is `6`. That's why they're called **enums**. They're *enumerated* values with names.

Using enums in this way has always been useful, but with Dart 2.17, they got even better. You can treat the new enhanced enums like classes. And that's what they are. Dart enums are subclasses of the `Enum` class. That means you can do many of the same things to enums that you would do with a class, including adding properties and methods, implementing interfaces and using mixins and generics.

Sound good? Get ready to enhance your enum skills then!

Reviewing the Basics

To get started, review what you already know about enums.

What to Use Enums For

Enums are great when you have a fixed number of options you want to represent. Here are some examples of that:

- Traffic light states (green, yellow, red).
- Days of the week (Monday, Tuesday, ...).
- Months of the year (January, February, ...).
- Audio playback states (playing, paused, ...).
- Weather types (sunny, cloudy, ...).

All these topics are more or less constant. People aren't going to be adding an eighth day of the week any time soon. Similarly, there are only a finite number of audio playback states. You could argue there are an indeterminate number of weather types, but if you've thought through your weather app carefully, you probably have a limited set that you need to show icons for.

On the other hand, when a category has frequent changes or an unlimited number of possibilities, this isn't a great choice for enums. Here are some examples of things you probably shouldn't represent with an enum:

- Users
- Songs
- URLs

If you add another song to your app, you'll probably have to refactor other parts of your code. For example, if you're handling the enum cases with `switch` statements, you have to update all the `switch` statements. So rather than enums, you'd be better off representing the data types listed above with classes you can store in a list. Then, whenever you add a new user or a new song, just add a new item to the list.

Advantages of Using Enums

In the past, people often wrote logic like this:

```
const int GREEN = 0;
const int YELLOW = 1;
const int RED = 2;

void printMessage(int lightColor) {
  switch (lightColor) {
    case GREEN:
      print('Go!');
      break;
    case YELLOW:
      print('Slow down!');
      break;
    case RED:
      print('Stop!');
      break;
    default:
      print('Unrecognized option');
  }
}
```

However, there were a few problems with this kind of logic:

- The function takes any integer, so if you had defined `int VOLUME = 2` somewhere else, there would be nothing to stop you from passing in `VOLUME` to the function, even though this function has nothing to do with volume.
- The compiler doesn't know there are only three possible options, so it can't warn you if you provide a value besides `0`, `1` or `2`. This requires you to handle error cases with `default`.
- Sometimes people used similar logic but with strings instead of integers. For example, `if (lightColor == 'green')`. With that method, it was easy to accidentally misspell values, such as writing `geen` instead of `green`.

Dart enums solve all those problems:

- Each enum has its own **namespace**, so there's no way to accidentally pass in `Audio.volume` when a function only accepts `TrafficLight` enum values.
- The Dart compiler is smart enough to know how many values an enum has. That means you don't need to use a default in a `switch` statement as long as you're already handling all the cases. Dart will also warn you if you aren't handling an enum case.

- The compiler tells you immediately if you misspell an enum value.

All in all, these features of enums make them a much better option than using integer or string constants as option markers.

Coding a Basic Enum

Can you write an enum for the colors of a traffic light?

Open a Dart project and add the following enum outside of `main`:

```
enum TrafficLight {
  green,
  yellow,
  red,
}
```

You use the `enum` keyword followed by the enum name in upper camel case. Curly braces enclose the comma-separated enum values. Adding a comma after the last item is optional but ensures that Dart will format the list vertically.

In `main`, use your `TrafficLight` enum like so:

```
final color = TrafficLight.green;
switch (color) {
  case TrafficLight.green:
    print('Go!');
    break;
  case TrafficLight.yellow:
    print('Slow down!');
    break;
  case TrafficLight.red:
    print('Stop!');
    break;
}
```

Dart recognizes that you're handling all the enum values, so no default case is necessary.

Run the code above, and you'll see `Go!` printed to the console.

That was a basic enum. Enhanced enums will allow you to simplify that code a lot. Keep reading to find out how.

Treating Enums Like Classes

Enums are just classes, and enum values are instances of the class. This means that you can apply much of your other knowledge about classes.

Adding Constructors and Properties

Just as classes have constructors and properties, so do enums.

Replace the `TrafficLight` enum you wrote earlier with the enhanced version:

```
enum TrafficLight {
  green('Go!'),
  yellow('Slow down!'),
  red('Stop!');

  const TrafficLight(this.message);
  final String message;
}
```

Here's what has changed:

- The enum has a `const` constructor, which it uses to set the final `message` field in the class. Enum constructors are always `const`.
- `green`, `yellow` and `red` are the only instances of the `TrafficLight` enum class. They each call the constructor and set the value of `message` for their instance.
- The last enum case, which is `red` in this example, ends with a semicolon. Commas still separate the other cases.

It's also permissible to keep the trailing comma, but you would still need to add a semicolon:

```
// alternate formatting
green('Go!'),
yellow('Slow down!'),
red('Stop!'),             // trailing comma
;                         // semicolon
```

The only advantage here is that you're explicitly telling the Dart formatter to display the enum list vertically rather than horizontally. Dart seems to do that anyway in this case, even without the trailing comma, so there's no need to add it. Carry on without making this change.

Now, your previous `switch` statement is no longer necessary. Replace the code in `main` with the following:

```
final color = TrafficLight.green;
print(color.message);
```

Your enum has a `message` parameter, which allows you to access the message directly. No need for `switch` statements. That's much better, isn't it?

Run your code, and you'll see the same message as before:

```
Go!
```

Operator Overloading

This is a good opportunity to teach you an aspect of classes you might not know about yet. The topic is **operator overloading**.

As you recall, operators are symbols like the following:

- Arithmetic operators: + −, ∗, /, ~/, %
- Equality and relational operators: ==, !=, >, <, >=, <=
- Assignment operators: =, +=, −=, ∗=, \=, ...
- Logical operators: !, &&, ||
- Bitwise and shift operators: &, |, ^, ~, >>, <<, >>>

These operators all have meanings in certain contexts. For example, when you use the + operator with integers, Dart adds them together:

```
print(3 + 2); // 5
```

When the context is strings, + has a different meaning:

```
print('a' + 'b'); // ab
```

In this case, Dart concatenates the two strings to produce ab.

However, what would it mean if you tried to add users, as in `user1 + user2`? In this context, Dart wouldn't know what to do because the + operator isn't defined for adding `User` classes.

You do have the opportunity to give your own meaning to operators when the context makes sense, though. This is called operator overloading. Many, though not all, of the operators you saw above support overloading.

The following example will show how to overload an operator in a normal class. After that, you'll see a second example where you can apply operator overloading to enums.

Overloading an Operator in a Class

Create the following `Point` class, which has x-y coordinates:

```
class Point {
  const Point(this.x, this.y);
  final double x;
  final double y;

  @override
  String toString() => '($x, $y)';
}
```

This class can represent points on a two-dimensional coordinate system where points are in the form `(x, y)`, such as `(1, 4)` or `(3, 2)`. The image below shows these on a graph where y is increasing in the downward direction, the usual orientation for rendering graphics:

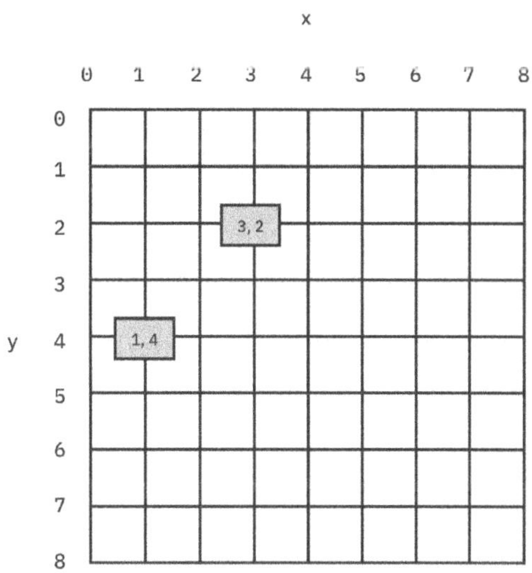

Two points on a graph

Implement these two points in code by writing the following in `main`:

```
const pointA = Point(1, 4);
const pointB = Point(3, 2);
```

In some situations, you might want to add two points together. You'd accomplish that by first adding the x-coordinates of the two points and then the y-coordinates. The following image shows the result:

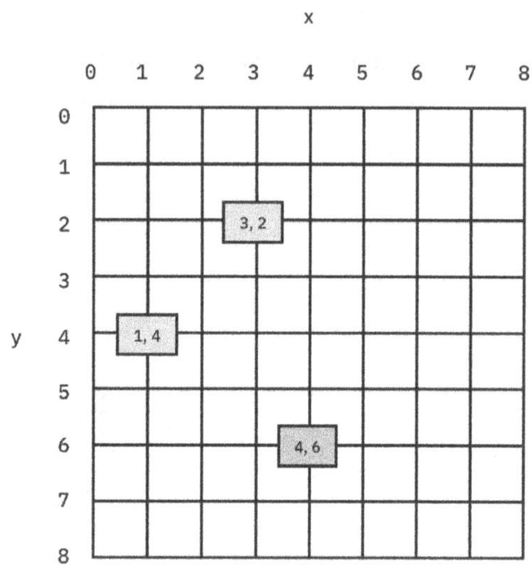

Two points added together

Dart doesn't know how to add two points, but you can tell Dart how to do it by overloading the + operator in your `Point` class.

Add the following code inside `Point`:

```
Point operator +(Point other) {
  return Point(x + other.x, y + other.y);
}
```

Here are a few points, hehe :], to note:

- Use the `operator` keyword when you want to overload an operator.
- Treat the operator as a method name. Because it *is* the method name. The + method is invoked on the first point: the point that comes before the +. The `other` point is the point that comes after the +.
- The `return` line creates a new point with the sum of the x-coordinates and the sum of the y-coordinates.

Now you can add points!

Add the following lines to the bottom of `main`:

```
final pointC = pointA + pointB;
print(pointC);
```

Run that, and you'll see the following result:

```
(4.0, 6.0)
```

Overloading an Operator in an Enum

Because enums are classes, they also support operator overloading.

Take the following enum for the days of the week as an example:

```
enum Day {
  monday,
  tuesday,
  wednesday,
  thursday,
  friday,
  saturday,
  sunday,
}
```

It might not make sense to add Monday plus Tuesday, but it sort of makes sense to say `monday + 2`. That would be two days later, right? Wednesday.

Replace the comma after `sunday` with a semicolon and add the + operator overload.

Here's the complete code:

```
enum Day {
  monday,
  tuesday,
  wednesday,
  thursday,
  friday,
  saturday,
  sunday;

  Day operator +(int days) {
    // 1
    final numberOfItems = Day.values.length;
    // 2
    final index = (this.index + days) % numberOfItems;
    // 3
    return Day.values[index];
  }
}
```

The numbered comments have the following notes:

1. `values` is a list of all the enum values, so `length` gives you the total number of values, which is 7 because there are seven days in a week.
2. The `index` is the enumerated value of each enum value. `monday` is `0`, `tuesday` is `1`, `wednesday` is 2 and so on. Because `this.index` is an integer, you can add `days` to it. The `%` modulo operator divides the result by 7 and gives the remainder. This makes the new `index` never go out of bounds, no matter how large `days` is. It will start over at the beginning of the list. `sunday + 1` is `monday` because `(6 + 1) % 7` is `0`.
3. Convert your newly calculated index back to an enum, and you're good to go.

To test it out, run the following code in `main`:

```
var day = Day.monday;

day = day + 2;
print(day.name); // wednesday

day += 4;
print(day.name); // sunday

day++;
print(day.name); // monday
```

Not only does the + operator work, you get += and ++ for free!

Adding Methods

You can also add methods to an enum just as you would to a normal class. Technically, operator overloading is already adding a method, but this section will provide an additional example.

Add the following getter method to your Day enum:

```
Day get next {
  return this + 1;
}
```

Because you already implemented support for the + operator, this method returns the next day by adding 1 to whatever value this day is.

Try it out in main like so:

```
final restDay = Day.saturday;
print(restDay.next);
```

Run that, and you'll see Day.sunday printed in the console.

Implementing Interfaces

Say you have the following interface that you use to serialize objects for storage in a database:

```
abstract class Serializable {
  String serialize();
}
```

As a reminder, "serializing" something just means to convert an object to a basic data type, most commonly a string.

Make an enum named Weather that implements the interface like so:

```
enum Weather implements Serializable {
  sunny,
  cloudy,
  rainy;

  @override
  String serialize() => name;
}
```

`serialize` directly returns the enum name, such as `'sunny'` or `'cloudy'`. The built-in `name` property is already a string.

Optionally, you can also add a deserialize method to your enum to go the other direction:

```
static Weather deserialize(String value) {
  return values.firstWhere(
    (element) => element.name == value,
    orElse: () => Weather.sunny,
  );
}
```

In contrast to the higher-order method `where` that you learned about in Chapter 2, "Anonymous Functions", `firstWhere` returns only a single value. By comparing the input `value` to the enum `name`, you convert the string back to an enum. If the string value doesn't exist, `orElse` will give you a default of `Weather.sunny`.

Use the methods in `main` like so:

```
final weather = Weather.cloudy;

String serialized = weather.serialize();
print(serialized);

Weather deserialized = Weather.deserialize(serialized);
print(deserialized);
```

Run this code to see the serialized string and the deserialized `Weather` object:

```
cloudy
Weather.cloudy
```

This example was merely to show you the syntax of implementing an interface. You could use these same methods without the interface, and it would all still work the same. The interface is only useful if some other part of your app requires `Serializable` objects.

> **Note**: Once you've serialized an enum, you can never change it again. Well, you can, but you do so at your peril. Say you've saved a bunch of enum values as strings in the database or sent them across the network. At that point, your enums have been released to the wild. You can't get them back because they're stored on user devices and far-away servers. If you change your enum in the next app update and then try to deserialize the old enum strings, you'll get mismatches and unexpected behavior. That's another reason you don't want to make enums out of things that change frequently.

Adding Mixins

If you have a bunch of different enums where you're repeating the same logic, you can simplify your code by adding a mixin.

Here's an example:

```
enum Fruit with Describer {
  cherry,
  peach,
  banana,
}

enum Vegetable with Describer {
  carrot,
  broccoli,
  spinach,
}

mixin Describer on Enum {
  void describe() {
    print('This $runtimeType is a $name.');
  }
}
```

Now, `Fruit` and `Vegetable` share the `describe` method. Using the `on` keyword in the mixin gave you access to the `name` property of the `Enum` class.

Test your mixin in `main` like so:

```
final fruit = Fruit.banana;
final vegi = Vegetable.broccoli;

fruit.describe();
vegi.describe();
```

Run that, and you'll see:

```
This Fruit is a banana.
This Vegetable is a broccoli.
```

OK, you English grammarians, so it shouldn't be "a broccoli" but just "broccoli". The author hadn't had dinner yet, and that's the best example he could think of.

Using Generics

Normally, all the values in an enum will be of the same type. For example, in the `Size` enum below, the `value` of each enum item is an `int`:

```
enum Size {
  small(1),
  medium(5),
  large(10);

  const Size(this.value);
  final int value;
}
```

However, you might want to store different types for each enum value in certain situations. Take the following example:

```
enum Default {
  font,
  size,
  weight,
}
```

Say you have some default values you want to associate with each enum value. The default font is "roboto", a `String`; the default size is 17.0, a `double`; and the default weight is 400, an `int`. Each enum value is a different instance of `Enum`. And when different instances use different types for their values, you need generics to handle them.

Replace the `Default` enum above with one that uses generics:

```
enum Default<T extends Object> {
  font<String>('roboto'),
  size<double>(17.0),
  weight<int>(400);

  const Default(this.value);
  final T value;
}
```

`Object` is the nearest common parent type of `String`, `double` and `int`, so the generic `T` type extends `Object`. This allows `value` to take any of those types. Remember that each enum value (`font`, `size` and `weight`) is an instance of the enum class. The type in angle brackets tells the constructor the type for that instance.

Write the following in `main`:

```
String defaultFont = Default.font.value;
double defaultSize = Default.size.value;
int defaultWeight = Default.weight.value;
```

Although there's only one `value` property in your enum, it resolves to a different type depending on the selected enum instance.

That wraps it up for this chapter. In the next chapter, you'll learn how to handle errors.

Challenges

Before moving on, here are some challenges to test your knowledge of enhanced enums. It's best if you try to solve them yourself, but solutions are available with the supplementary materials for this book if you get stuck.

Challenge 1: Better Days Ahead

In this chapter, you wrote a `Day` enum with the seven days of the week.

1. Override the - operator so you can subtract integers from enum values.
2. When you print the `name` of your `Day` enum, it prints the days of the week in all lowercase. It's standard to use lower camel case for enum values, but it would be nice to use uppercase for the display name. For example, `Monday` instead of `monday`. Add a `displayName` property to `Day` for that.

Challenge 2: Not Found, 404

Create an enum for HTTP response status codes. The enum should have properties for the code and the meaning. For example, `404` and `'Not Found'`. If you aren't familiar with the HTTP codes, look them up online. You don't need to cover every possible code, just a few of the common ones.

Key Points

- Dart enums are subclasses of `Enum`.
- Enums are good for representing a fixed number of options.
- Prefer enums over strings or integers as option markers.
- Enhanced enums support constructors, properties, methods, operator overloading, interfaces, mixins and generics.
- Enums must have `const` constructors.
- The enum values are instances of the enum class.
- Operator overloading allows classes to give their own definitions to some operators.

Chapter 10: Error Handling

By Jonathan Sande

It's natural to only code the happy path as you begin to work on a project.

- *"This text input will always be a valid email address."*
- *"The internet is always connected."*
- *"That function's return value is always a positive integer."*

Until it isn't.

When a baker makes a mistake, cookies get burned. When an author makes a mistake, words get mispelled. Eaters will swallow and readers overlook, but code doesn't forgive. Maybe you noticed misspelled was "*mispelled*" in the previous sentence. Or maybe you missed it. We all make mistakes, but when a programmer makes one, the whole app crashes. That's the nature of a programmer's work. The purpose of this chapter is to teach you how to crash a little less.

Errors and Exceptions in Dart

The creators of Dart had such confidence you and your users would make mistakes that they built error handling right into the language. Before you learn how to handle errors, though, you get to make them!

How to Crash an App

You have many ways to cause your application to give up all hope of survival and quit. Open a new project and try out a few of them.

Dividing by Zero

One way to crash is to divide by zero. You learned in elementary school that you can't do that.

Write the following code in `main`:

```
1 ~/ 0;
```

Remember, ~/ is for integer division. The expression `1 / 0` is floating-point division and would give you a result of `double.infinity` without crashing.

Now, run your code *without* debugging. There are a few ways to do that:

- Choose **Run ▸ Run Without Debugging** from the menu.
- Click **Run**, not Debug, above the `main` method:

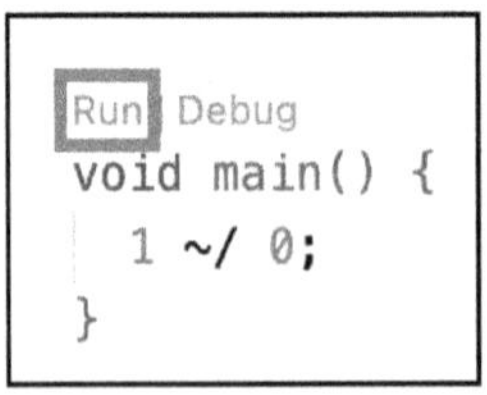

- In the top-right of the window, click the dropdown menu next to the **Run** button and make sure it says **Run Without Debugging**:

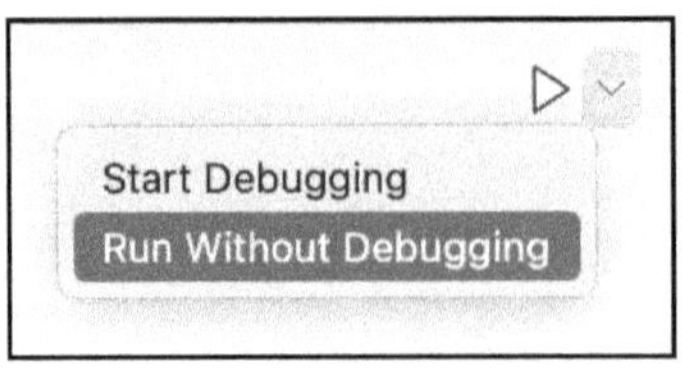

> **Note**: You'll learn about debugging later in this chapter, but until directed to do differently, run all the examples here without debugging. That way, VS Code won't pause when it reaches an error.

After running the program, check the debug console to see an error message that begins with the following two lines:

```
Unhandled exception:
IntegerDivisionByZeroException
```

`IntegerDivisionByZeroException` is Dart's name for what happened. An **exception** is something outside of the usual rules. Dividing by an integer is normal, but dividing by zero is an *exceptional* case. Even though it's exceptional, you're still expected to know and plan for it. Not handling an exception is an **error**. And errors crash your app.

> **Note**: Sometimes you'll see the words "error" and "exception" used interchangeably, but strictly speaking, an exception is typical and good when properly handled, whereas an error is bad.

No Such Method

In the past, you often got a `NoSuchMethodError` when you forgot to handle `null` values. Because the `Null` class doesn't have many methods, almost anything you tried to do with `null` caused this crash.

After Dart added sound null safety, `NoSuchMethodErrors` became far less common. You can still see what it looks like by turning off type checking using `dynamic`.

Write the following in `main`:

```
dynamic x = null;
print(x.isEven);
```

Unlike integers, `null` doesn't have an `isEven` getter method. So when you run that code, you get the following message:

```
Unhandled exception:
NoSuchMethodError: The getter 'isEven' was called on null.
```

The error you got here was a **runtime error**. Dart didn't discover it until you ran the code.

Change `dynamic` to `int` in the code above:

```
int x = null;
print(x.isEven);
```

Now, you have a **compile-time error**. VS Code puts little red squiggles under `null` with the message that you're not allowed to do that:

```
int x = null;
```

```
A value of type 'Null' can't be assigned to a variable of type
'int'.
```

Compile-time errors are much better than runtime errors because they're obvious and immediate.

Format Exception

Another way to crash your app is to try and decode a "JSON" string that isn't actually in JSON format.

Replace the contents of your project file with the following code:

```
import 'dart:convert';

void main() {
  const malformedJson = 'abc';
  jsonDecode(malformedJson);
}
```

The string `'abc'` isn't in JSON format, so when you try to decode it, you get the following error message:

```
Unhandled exception:
FormatException: Unexpected character (at character 1)
abc
^
```

This is a format exception, which Dart identifies with the `FormatException` class.

Another way to cause a format exception is to try to turn a non-numeric string into an integer:

```
int.parse('42');    // OK
int.parse('hello'); // FormatException
```

The first line is fine. It converts the string `'42'` into the integer 42. However, Dart has no idea how to convert the string `'hello'` into an integer, so it stops executing the program with the following error:

```
Unhandled exception:
FormatException: Invalid radix-10 number (at character 1)
hello
^
```

"Radix-10" means base-10 or decimal, as opposed to binary or hexadecimal numbers, which `parse` also supports. `hello` wouldn't work in binary or hex either, but come to think of it, `DAD`, `FED`, `BEEF`, `DEAD`, `C0FFEE` *would* parse in hex.

There are many other ways to crash your app. But hopefully, the examples above gave you a taste of how to do it. As if anyone needed help with this kind of thing.

Reading Stack Traces

The sections above only gave you part of the error messages. You probably noticed that the full message was much longer and a lot of it looked like unintelligible gibberish. The unintelligible part is called a stack trace:

```
Unhandled exception:
FormatException: Invalid radix-10 number (at character 1)
hello
^

#0      int._handleFormatError (dart:core-patch/integers_patch.dart:131:5)
#1      int._parseRadix (dart:core-patch/integers_patch.dart:142:16)
#2      int._parse (dart:core-patch/integers_patch.dart:103:12)
#3      int.parse (dart:core-patch/integers_patch.dart:65:12)
#4      main                                        bin/starter.dart:3
#5      _delayEntrypointInvocation.<anonymous closure> (dart:isolate-patch/isolate_patch.da
rt:297:19)
#6      _RawReceivePortImpl._handleMessage (dart:isolate-patch/isolate_patch.dart:192:12)

Exited (255)
```

Stack trace

A **stack trace** is a printout of all the methods on the call stack when an error occurs. In the stack trace above, most methods are internal. `#4 main` is the only one that's part of your code.

Do you remember the stack data structure you made for the challenges in Chapter 8, "Generics"? Well, it turns out stacks are pretty important in computer science. Computers use them to keep track of the current method being executed.

To see this more clearly, write some functions that call other functions:

```
void main() {
  functionOne();
}

void functionOne() {
  functionTwo();
}

void functionTwo() {
  functionThree();
}

void functionThree() {
  int.parse('hello');
}
```

When Dart executes this program, it'll start by calling `main`. Because `main` is the current function, Dart adds `main` to the **call stack**. You can think of a stack like a stack of pancakes. `main` is the first pancake on the stack. Then, `main` calls `functionOne`, so Dart puts `functionOne` on the call stack. `functionOne` is the second pancake on the stack. `functionOne` calls `functionTwo`, and `functionTwo` calls `functionThree`. Each time you enter a new function, Dart adds it to the call stack.

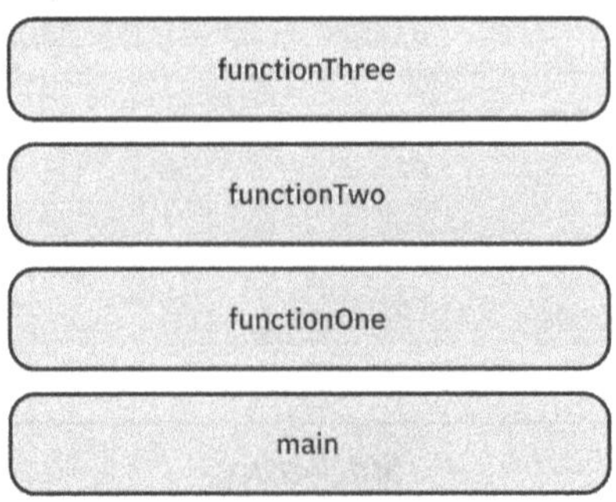

Call stack

Normally, when `functionThree` finishes, Dart would pop it off the top of the stack, go back to `functionTwo`, finish `functionTwo`, pop it off the stack and so on until `main` finishes. However, in this case, there's about to be a tragedy in `functionThree`, which will bring everything to a grinding halt.

Run the code you just wrote. The app crashes when you reach the line `int.parse('hello');`. Look at the debug console, and you'll see the stack trace that shows the call stack at the time of the crash.

```
#0      int._handleFormatError (dart:core-patch/integers_patch.dart:131:5)
#1      int._parseRadix (dart:core-patch/integers_patch.dart:142:16)
#2      int._parse (dart:core-patch/integers_patch.dart:103:12)
#3      int.parse (dart:core-patch/integers_patch.dart:65:12)
#4      functionThree                                bin/starter.dart:14
#5      functionTwo                                  bin/starter.dart:10
#6      functionOne                                   bin/starter.dart:6
#7      main                                          bin/starter.dart:2
#8      _delayEntrypointInvocation.<anonymous closure> (dart:isolate-patch/
isolate_patch.dart:297:19)
#9      _RawReceivePortImpl._handleMessage (dart:isolate-patch/isolate_patc
h.dart:192:12)
```

Stack trace

There, your four methods sit in the middle of the stack. The other methods above and below them are internal to Dart. On the right side, you can see **bin/starter.dart** followed by a line number. Yours might look different if your project name is different. Click the one after `functionThree`, and VS Code brings you to the line number where the crash occurred in `functionThree`, at `int.parse('hello');`.

Stack traces look messy and intimidating, but they're your friends. They hold some of the first clues to what went wrong.

Debugging

It's not always obvious from the stack trace where the bug in your code is. VS Code has good debugging tools to help you out in this situation.

Writing Some Buggy Code

Replace your project file with the following code:

```
void main() {
  final characters = ' abcdefghijklmnopqrstuvwxyz';
  final data = [4, 1, 18, 20, 0, 9, 19, 0, 6, 21, 14, 27];
  final buffer = StringBuffer();
  for (final index in data) {
    final letter = characters[index];
    buffer.write(letter);
  }
  print(buffer);
}
```

First, run the code without debugging. You'll get a crash with the following error message:

```
Unhandled exception:
RangeError (index): Invalid value: Not in inclusive range 0..26: 27
#0      _StringBase.[] (dart:core-patch/string_patch.dart:260:41)
#1      main                                                    bin/starter.dart:6
#2      _delayEntrypointInvocation.<anonymous closure> (dart:isolate-patch/isolate_patch.dart:297:19)
#3      _RawReceivePortImpl._handleMessage (dart:isolate-patch/isolate_patch.dart:192:12)
```

Hmm, what does that mean?

The stack trace tells you the error happened in the `main` method on line 6, which is the following line:

```
final letter = characters[index];
```

That line looks OK — no division by zero or trying to parse a weird string.

To find the error, you'll use the debugging tools available in VS Code and step through your code line by line.

Adding a Breakpoint

Click the margin to the left of line 2. This will add a red dot:

```
   Run | Debug
1  void main() {
2    final characters = ' abcdefghijklmnopqrstuvwxyz';
3    final data = [4, 1, 18, 20, 0, 9, 19, 0, 6, 21, 14, 27];
4    final buffer = StringBuffer();
5    for (final index in data) {
6      final letter = characters[index];
7      buffer.write(letter);
8    }
9    print(buffer);
10 }
11
```

Breakpoint on line 2

That red dot is called a **breakpoint**. When you run your app in debug mode, execution will pause when it reaches that line.

Running in Debug Mode

Now, start your app in debug mode. Like before, there are a few ways to do that:

- Choose **Run ▸ Start Debugging** from the menu.
- Click **Debug** above the `main` method:

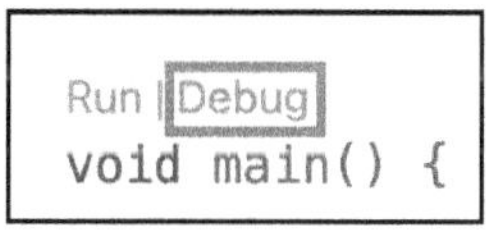

- In the top-right of the window, click the dropdown menu next to the **Run** button and make sure it says **Start Debugging**:

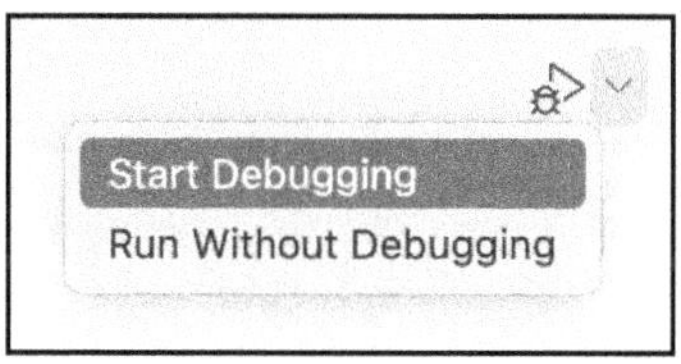

Stepping Over the Code Line by Line

VS Code pauses execution at line 2. Then, a floating button bar pops up with various debugging options. If you hover your mouse over each button, you can see what it does. The most important ones for now are the two on the left:

- **Continue**: This is the button with the line and triangle. It resumes normal execution until the next breakpoint, if any, is reached.

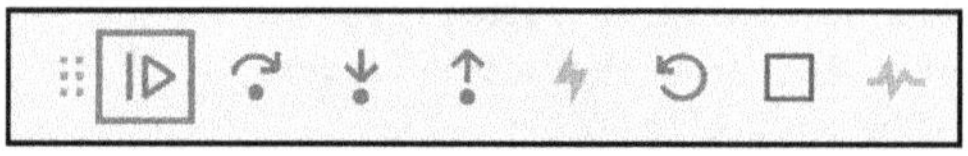

- **Step Over**: This is the clockwise arrow over the dot. Pressing it executes one line of code but doesn't descend into the body of any function it reaches. That's fine because you don't have other functions besides `main` in this example.

> **Note**: Later, when you're debugging an app with functions, use the **Step Into** button, the one with the arrow pointing down at the dot, to enter the body of another function. For example, if you wanted to follow the logic of the recursive functions in Chapter 8, "Generics", you would use this button.

Press the **Step Over** button several times until execution reaches **line 7**: `buffer.write(letter);`.

Look at the **Run and Debug** panel on the left. The **Variables** section shows the current values of the variables in your code.

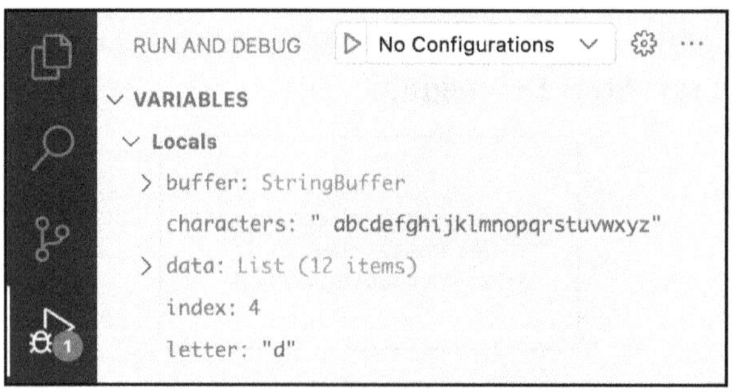

Run and Debug panel: Variables

Keep pressing **Step Over** for a few more iterations of the `for` loop while keeping an eye on the values of the variables. You'll begin to see the pattern of how the code works. Stepping through code one line at a time like this will often help you discover even the hardest-to-find bugs.

Watching Expressions

When you tire of stepping one line at a time through the `for` loop, add a breakpoint to **line 6**: `final letter = characters[index];`.

Then, find the **Watch** section on the **Run and Debug** panel. Add the following two expressions by pressing the + button:

- `characters[index]`
- `buffer.toString()`

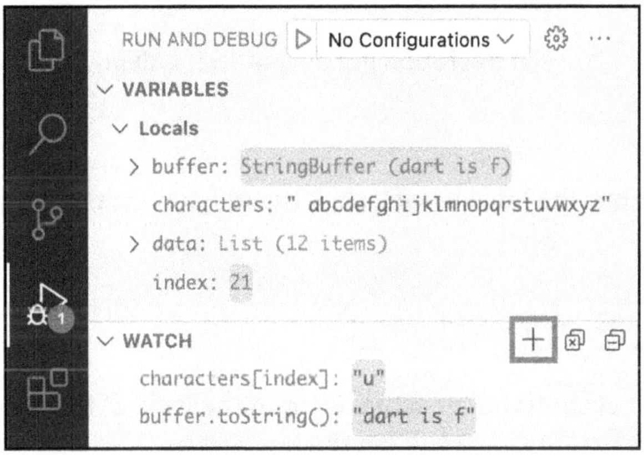

Adding a Watch expression

After that, press the **Continue** button a few times, keeping an eye on the expressions you're watching on the left.

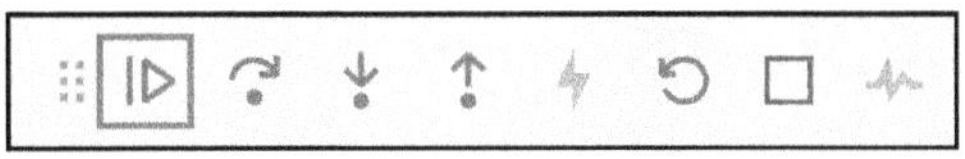

Fixing the Bug

When the app finally crashes, what's the value of `index`?

It's 27. What's the length of the `characters` string? If you don't want to count, add `characters.length` to the Watch window. It's also 27.

Ah, that's it! You recall that lists and string indexes are 0-based, so index 27 is one greater than the last position in the list. That was causing the range error.

You remember that you wanted to end the message with an exclamation mark but forgot to add it to `characters`.

If your code is still running, press the **Stop** button:

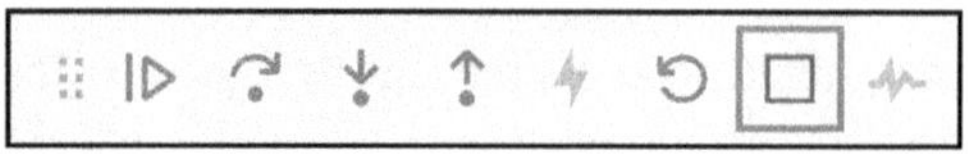

Then, replace line 2 with the following:

```
final characters = ' abcdefghijklmnopqrstuvwxyz!';
```

Note the `!` at the end of the string.

Now, rerun the code without debugging.

No errors this time! You see the following output in the debug console:

```
dart is fun!
```

If you want to remove the breakpoints, click the red dots on the left of lines 2 and 6.

Handling Exceptions

The bug in the last section was an actual error in the logic of the code. There was no way to handle that except to track down the bug and fix it.

Other types of crashes, though, are caused by valid exceptions that you aren't properly handling. You need to think about these and how to deal with them.

Catching Exceptions

As you saw earlier, one source of these exceptions is invalid JSON. When connected to the internet, you can't control what comes to you from the outside world. Invalid JSON doesn't happen very often, but you should write code to deal with it when you get it.

Replace your project file with the following code:

```
import 'dart:convert';

void main() {
  const json = 'abc';

  try {
    dynamic result = jsonDecode(json);
    print(result);
  } catch (e) {
    print('There was an error.');
    print(e);
  }
}
```

Here are a few comments:

- In Chapter 12, "Futures", you'll learn how to retrieve JSON strings from the internet. For now, though, you're just using a hard-coded string for the JSON.
- The new code is a `try-catch` block. You put the code that might **throw an exception** in the `try` block. Yes, it's called "throw", but the meaning is "cause". If it does throw, the `catch` block will handle the exception without crashing the app. In this case, all you're doing is printing a message and the error.
- Here, e is the error or exception. You can use `catch (e, s)` instead if you need the stack trace, s being the `StackTrace` object.

Run the code, and you'll see the following result:

```
There was an error.
FormatException: Unexpected character (at character 1)
abc
^
```

Unlike when you had a `FormatException` earlier in the lesson, this time, the app didn't crash. You *handled* this exception.

> **Note**: In a real app, you'd want to do more than print the error message. In fact, you should remove `print` statements from production apps because they can sometimes leak sensitive data.
>
> How to handle this particular exception would depend on the context. Say a user requested to see some song lyrics, so your app asked the server for them but got back invalid JSON. What should you do in this case? Probably, you'd want to notify the user that the song lyrics they requested aren't currently available.

In the code above, replace this line:

```
const json = 'abc';
```

With the following line containing a valid JSON string:

```
const json = '{"name":"bob"}';
```

Then, rerun the code. This time, the `try` block finishes successfully, and you see the Dart map that `jsonFormat` produced:

```
{name: bob}
```

Handling Specific Exceptions

Using a `catch` block will catch every exception that happens in the `try` block.

"Perfect!" you say. "I'll just wrap my entire app in one big `try-catch` block. No more crashes!"

Even though that might sound like a good idea, `try-catch` isn't magic. It doesn't make the problems go away. In fact, sometimes, it can make things worse because you're hiding your problems rather than dealing with them. Sometimes coding can be like real life, can't it?

Just as you can't solve your life troubles all at once, you can't handle every programming exception with one `catch` block. It's better to focus on one problem at a time, both in life and in coding.

To catch a specific exception, use the on keyword. Replace the body of `main` with the following code:

```
const json = 'abc';

try {
  dynamic result = jsonDecode(json);
  print(result);
} on FormatException {
  print('The JSON string was invalid.');
}
```

Now, it's very clear that you're only handling format exceptions.

Run the code, and you'll see the expected message:

```
The JSON string was invalid.
```

You're handling format exceptions, but if there are any other exceptions, your app will still crash.

"What?" you say. "I don't want my app to crash! Please just let me use a `catch` block."

If you don't know what you're catching, how can you handle it? After all, the solution to no internet is quite different than the solution to a range error. If the app crashes, that's a good thing. It's a loud and clear signal that there's an exceptional situation happening that you need to know about.

Handling Multiple Exceptions

When there's more than one potential exception that could occur, you can use multiple on blocks to target them.

Replace your project file with the following example:

```
void main() {
  const numberStrings = ["42", "hello"];

  try {
    for (final numberString in numberStrings) {
      final number = int.parse(numberString);
      print(number ~/ 0);
    }
  } on FormatException {
    handleFormatException();
  } on UnsupportedError {
```

```
      handleDivisionByZero();
    }
  }

  void handleFormatException() {
    print("You tried to parse a non-numeric string.");
  }

  void handleDivisionByZero() {
    print("You can't divide by zero.");
  }
```

Here are some notes:

- This time, you're handling two possible errors. The extra functions emphasize that you can break your handling code into separate logical units.
- `IntegerDivisionByZeroException` is deprecated and will probably be removed from the language in the future. That doesn't mean you'll be able to divide by zero in the future. It just means you should call it `UnsupportedError` when catching such an exception.

Run the code above to see the result:

```
You can't divide by zero.
```

The code in the `try` block terminates as soon as you hit the first error. You never made it to the format exception. But you were ready for it.

The Finally Block

There's also a `finally` block you can add to your `try-catch` structure. The code in that block runs both if the `try` block is successful and if the `catch` or `on` block catches an exception.

Replace the contents of `main` with the following example:

```
void main() {
  final database = FakeDatabase();
  database.open();

  try {
    final data = database.fetchData();
    final number = int.parse(data);
    print('The number is $number.');
  } on FormatException {
    print("Dart didn't recognize that as a number.");
```

```
  } finally {
    database.close();
  }
}

class FakeDatabase {
  void open() => print('Opening the database.');
  void close() => print('Closing the database.');
  String fetchData() => 'forty-two';
}
```

`FakeDatabase` represents a situation where you must clean up some resources even if the operation in the `try` block is unsuccessful. Note that you "close" the database in the `finally` block.

Run the code to see the result:

```
Opening the database.
Dart didn't recognize that as a number.
Closing the database.
```

The `try` block failed because parsing `forty-two` threw a format exception. Even so, the database still had an opportunity to close.

Now, replace `'forty-two'` in the code above with `'42'`. Then, rerun the program.

This time, you'll see:

```
Opening the database.
The number is 42.
Closing the database.
```

The `try` block was successful, and the `finally` block also ran its code.

Writing Custom Exceptions

You should use the standard exceptions whenever you can, but you can also define your own exceptions when appropriate.

Back in Chapter 1, "String Manipulation", you learned how to validate passwords with regular expressions. You'll build on that foundation now by defining some custom exceptions for invalid passwords.

Defining the Exceptions

First, create the following `Exception` class for passwords that are too short:

```
class ShortPasswordException implements Exception {
  ShortPasswordException(this.message);
  final String message;
}
```

As you can see, it's pretty easy to make a custom exception. All you need to do is implement `Exception` and create a field that will hold a message describing the problem.

Create a few more exceptions for other password problems:

```
class NoNumberException implements Exception {
  NoNumberException(this.message);
  final String message;
}

class NoUppercaseException implements Exception {
  NoUppercaseException(this.message);
  final String message;
}

class NoLowercaseException implements Exception {
  NoLowercaseException(this.message);
  final String message;
}
```

Those are exceptions you can throw if the potential password doesn't include a number, uppercase letter or lowercase letter.

Throwing Exceptions

Now, add the following validation method below `main`:

```
void validateLength(String password) {
  final goodLength = RegExp(r'.{12,}');
  if (!password.contains(goodLength)) {
    throw ShortPasswordException('Password must be at least 12
characters!');
  }
}
```

Use the `throw` keyword when you want to throw an exception. You can throw anything. For example, you could even throw a string and it would halt program execution if you didn't handle it:

```
throw 'rotten tomatoes';
```

But it's better that you throw classes that implement `Exception`.

Add a few more validation methods below `main`:

```
void validateLowercase(String password) {
  final lowercase = RegExp(r'[a-z]');
  if (!password.contains(lowercase)) {
    throw NoLowercaseException('Password must have a lowercase
letter!');
  }
}

void validateUppercase(String password) {
  final uppercase = RegExp(r'[A-Z]');
  if (!password.contains(uppercase)) {
    throw NoUppercaseException('Password must have an uppercase
letter!');
  }
}

void validateNumber(String password) {
  final number = RegExp(r'[0-9]');
  if (!password.contains(number)) {
    throw NoNumberException('Password must have a number!');
  }
}
```

Those throw the other exceptions you made.

Now, create one more validation function to combine the others:

```
void validatePassword(String password) {
  validateLength(password);
  validateLowercase(password);
  validateUppercase(password);
  validateNumber(password);
}
```

You could have put all the earlier validation logic right here in this function. However, the **Single Responsibility Principle** says that a function should do only one thing. Extracting code into short and simple functions makes the logic easier to reason about. Writing clean code is a step in the right direction toward preventing errors. And preventing errors is better than handling them!

Handling Custom Exceptions

Now that you have all the exceptions defined and the validation logic set up, you're ready to use them. Replace the contents of `main` with the following code:

```
const password = 'password1234';

try {
  validatePassword(password);
  print('Password is valid');
} on ShortPasswordException catch (e) {
  print(e.message);
} on NoLowercaseException catch (e) {
  print(e.message);
} on NoUppercaseException catch (e) {
  print(e.message);
} on NoNumberException catch (e) {
  print(e.message);
}
```

In addition to demonstrating how to use your custom exceptions, this example shows that you can combine the `on` and `catch` keywords. The `e` is an instance of your custom exception class, giving you access to the `message` property you defined.

Run the code to see the message:

```
Password must have an uppercase letter!
```

Play around with the password to confirm that the other exceptions work as well.

Challenges

Before moving on, here are some challenges to test your knowledge of error handling. It's best if you try to solve them yourself, but solutions are available with the supplementary materials for this book if you get stuck.

Challenge 1: Double the Fun

Here's a list of strings. Try to parse each of them with `double.parse`. Handle any format exceptions that occur.

```
final numbers = ['3', '1E+8', '1.25', 'four', '-0.01', 'NaN',
'Infinity'];
```

Challenge 2: Five Digits, No More, No Less

- Create a custom exception named `InvalidPostalCode`.
- Validate that a postal code is five digits.
- If it isn't, throw the exception.

Key Points

- An error is something that crashes your app.
- An exception is a known situation you must plan for and handle.
- Not handling an exception is an error.
- A stack trace is a crash report that tells you the method and line that crashed your app.
- VS Code debugging tools allow you to set breakpoints and execute your code one line at a time.
- `try/catch` blocks are one way to handle exceptions.
- It's better to handle specific exceptions with the `on` keyword rather than blindly handling all exceptions with `catch`.
- If you have a logic error in your app, don't "handle" it with `catch`. Let your app crash and then fix the bug.
- Add a `finally` block to `try-catch` if you need to clean up resources.
- You can create custom exceptions that implement `Exception`.

Where to Go From Here?

It's a good thing when your app crashes while developing it. That's a signal of something you need to fix. But when your app crashes for your users after you've published it, that's not such a good thing. Some people might email you when they find a bug. Others might leave a negative review online, but most users won't tell you about crashes or bugs. For that reason, you might consider using a **third-party crash reporting** library in your app. It'll collect crash reports in a central location. Analyzing those reports will help you find and fix bugs you wouldn't otherwise know about.

Another important topic you should learn about is **unit testing**. Unit testing is where you write code to test your app's individual units of logic. These units are usually classes or functions. Systematic testing ensures that all the logic in your app behaves as expected. Going through this process will not only help you discover hidden bugs, it'll also keep you from breaking things in the future that used to work in the past. That's called a **regression bug**.

Chapter 11: Concurrency

By Jonathan Sande

Your computer does a lot of work and does it so fast that you don't usually realize how much it's doing. Now and then, though — especially on an older computer or phone — you might notice an app slow down or even freeze. This might express itself during an animation as **jank**: that annoying stutter that happens when the device does so much work that some animation frames get dropped.

Long-running tasks generally fall into two categories: I/O tasks and computationally intensive tasks. I/O, or input-output, includes reading and writing files, accessing a database or downloading content from the internet. These all happen outside the CPU, so the CPU has to wait for them to complete. On the other hand, computationally intensive tasks happen inside the CPU. These tasks might include decrypting data, performing a mathematical calculation or parsing JSON.

As a developer, you must consider how your app, and particularly your UI, will respond when it meets these time-consuming tasks. Can you imagine if a user clicked a download button in your app, and the app froze until the 20 MB download was complete? You'd be collecting one-star reviews in a hurry.

Thankfully, Dart has a powerful solution baked into the very core of the language, allowing you to handle delays gracefully without blocking your app's responsiveness.

Concurrency in Dart

A **thread** is a sequence of commands that a computer executes. Some programming languages support multithreading — running multiple threads simultaneously — but others don't. Dart is a single-threaded language.

"What? Was it designed back in 1990 or something?"

No, Dart was created in 2011, well into the age of multicore CPUs.

"What a waste of all those other processing cores!"

Ah, but no. The developers deliberately made Dart single-threaded, providing significant advantages, as you'll soon see.

Parallelism vs. Concurrency

To understand Dart's model for handling long-running tasks and to see why Dart's creators decided to make Dart single-threaded, it helps to understand the difference between parallelism and concurrency. In common English, these words mean about the same thing, but a distinction exists in computer science.

Parallelism is when multiple tasks run *at the same time* on multiple processors or CPU cores; **concurrency** is when multiple tasks take turns running on a single CPU core. When a restaurant has a single person alternately taking orders and clearing tables, that's concurrency. But a restaurant that has one person taking orders and a different person clearing tables, that's parallelism.

"It seems like parallelism is better."

It can be — when there's a lot of work to do and that work is easily split into independent tasks. However, parallelism has some disadvantages, too.

A Problem With Parallelism

Little Susie has four pieces of chocolate left in the box next to her bed. She used to have ten, but she's already eaten six of them. She's saved the best ones for last because three friends are coming home with her after school today. She can't wait to share the chocolates with them. Imagine her horror, though, when she gets home and finds only two pieces of chocolate left in the box! After a lengthy investigation, it turns out that Susie's brother had discovered the stash and helped himself to two of the chocolates. From then on, Susie locked the box whenever she left home.

The same thing can happen in parallel threads with access to the same memory. One thread saves a value in memory and expects the value to be the same when the thread checks the value later. However, if a second thread modifies the value, the first thread gets confused. It can be a major headache to track down those kinds of bugs because they come from a source completely separate from the code that reports the error. A language that supports multithreading needs to set up a system of locks so values won't change at the wrong time. The cognitive load of designing, implementing and debugging a system with multiple threads can be heavy.

So the problem isn't with parallelism but rather with multiple threads having access to the same state in memory.

Dart Isolates

Dart's single thread runs in what it calls an **isolate**. Each isolate has its own allocated memory, ensuring that no isolate can access any other isolate's state. That means there's no need for a complicated locking system. It also means sensitive data is much more secure. Such a system greatly reduces the cognitive load on a programmer.

"But isn't concurrency slow?"

If you're running all of a program's tasks on a single thread, it seems like it would be really slow. However, it turns out that's not usually the case.

In the following image, you can see multiple tasks running on two threads in parallel. A rectangle represents each task, and longer rectangles represent longer-running tasks. A flat line represents an idle state where the thread isn't doing anything:

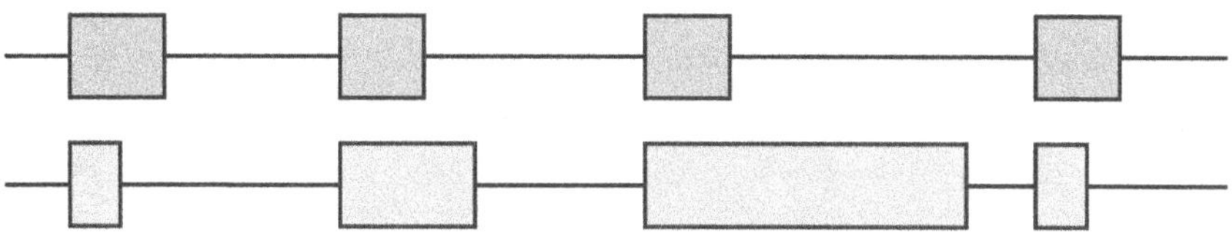

Processing tasks in parallel

The next image shows the same tasks running concurrently on a single thread:

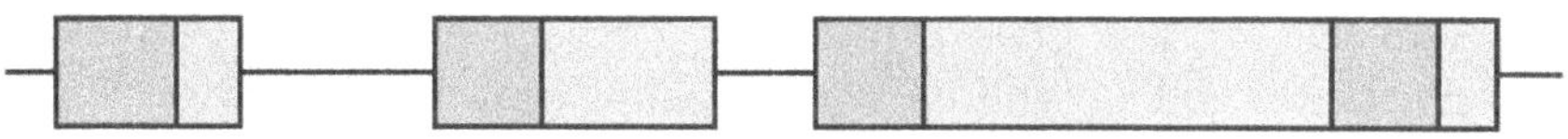

Processing tasks concurrently

The concurrent version does take a little longer, but it isn't *much longer*. The reason is that the parallel threads were idle for much of the time. A single thread is usually more than enough to accomplish what needs to be done.

Flutter has to update the UI 60 times a second. Each update timeslice is called a **frame**. That leaves about 16 milliseconds to redraw the UI on each frame. It typically doesn't take that long, giving you time to perform other work while the thread is idle. The user won't notice any problems as long as that work doesn't block Flutter from updating the UI on the next frame. The trick is to schedule tasks during the thread's downtimes.

Synchronous vs. Asynchronous Code

The word **synchronous** consists of *syn*, meaning "together", and *chron*, meaning "time", thus *together in time*. Synchronous code executes each instruction in order, one line of code immediately following the previous one.

This contrasts with **asynchronous** code, which means *not* together in time. Asynchronous code reschedules certain tasks to run in the future when the thread isn't busy.

All the code you've written so far in the book has been synchronous. For example:

```
print('first');
print('second');
print('third');
```

Run that, and it prints:

```
first
second
third
```

Because the code executes synchronously, it'll never print in a different order like `third first second`.

For many tasks, order matters:

- You have to open the bottle before you can take a drink.
- You have to turn on the car before you can drive it.
- Multiplying before adding is different than adding before multiplying.

For other tasks, though, the order doesn't matter:

- It doesn't matter if you brush your teeth first or wash your face first.
- It doesn't matter if you put a sock on the right foot first or the left foot first.

As in life, so it is with Dart. Although some code must execute in order, other tasks can be temporarily postponed. The postponable tasks are where the Dart event loop comes in.

The Event Loop

You've learned that Dart employs concurrency on a single thread, but how does Dart manage to schedule tasks asynchronously? Dart uses what it calls an **event loop** to execute tasks that had been postponed.

The event loop uses a data structure called a **queue**. Think of a queue like waiting in line at the grocery store. When you first join the line, you stand at the back of the line. Then, you slowly move to the front of the line as people before you leave. The first one in line is the first to leave. For that reason, developers call a queue a first-in-first-out, or FIFO, data structure. Dart uses queues to schedule tasks to execute on the main isolate.

The event loop has two queues: an **event queue** and a **microtask queue**. The event queue is for events like a user touching the screen or data coming in from a remote server. Dart primarily uses the microtask queue internally to prioritize certain small tasks that can't wait for the tasks in the event queue to finish.

Look at the following image:

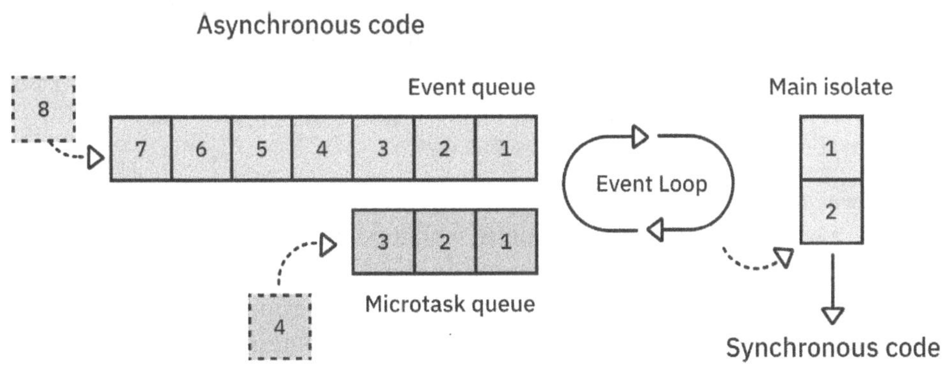

- Synchronous tasks in the main isolate thread are always run immediately. You can't interrupt them.

- If Dart finds any long-running tasks that agree to be postponed, Dart puts them in the event queue.
- When Dart finishes running the synchronous tasks, the event loop checks the microtask queue. If the microtask queue has any tasks, the event loop puts them on the main thread to execute next. The event loop keeps checking the microtask queue until it's empty.
- If the synchronous tasks and microtask queue are both empty, the event loop sends the next waiting task in the event queue to run on the main thread. Once it gets there, the code executes synchronously. Like any other synchronous code, nothing can interrupt it after it starts.
- If new microtasks enter the microtask queue, the event loop handles them before the next event in the event queue.
- This process continues until all the queues are empty.

Typically, if all the tasks are finished, this would indicate that it's time to exit the main isolate and terminate the application. However, the isolate will stay around if it's waiting for a response from the outside world. Maybe that's a timer that the isolate previously started, or perhaps it's listening for a response from a user or remote server.

Running Code in Parallel

When people say Dart is single-threaded, they mean Dart only runs on a single thread in the isolate. However, that *doesn't* mean you can't have tasks running on another thread. One example of this is when the underlying platform performs some work at the request of Dart. For example, when you ask to read a file on the system, that work isn't happening on the Dart thread. The system is doing the work inside its own process. Once the system finishes its work, it passes the result back to Dart, and Dart schedules some code to handle the result in the event queue. A lot of the I/O work from the `dart:io` library happens this way.

Another way to perform work on other threads is to create a new Dart isolate. The new isolate has its own memory and thread working in parallel with the main isolate. The two isolates are only able to communicate through messages, though. They have no access to each other's memory state. The idea is like messaging a friend. Sending your friend a text message doesn't give you access to the internal memory of their mobile device. They simply check their messages and reply to you when they feel like it.

You won't often need to create a new isolate. However, if you have a task that's taking too long on your main isolate thread, which you'll notice as unresponsiveness or jank in the UI, then this work is likely a good candidate for handing it off to another isolate. Chapter 14, "Isolates", will teach you how to do that.

Observing the Event Loop

Theory is nice, but it's time for some cold, hard code. In this chapter, you'll use the `Future` class to observe the event loop by adding tasks to the event and microtask queues. In Chapter 12, "Futures", you'll learn to use `Future` for more practical applications.

Adding a Task to the Event Queue

Passing a block of code to `Future` causes Dart to put that code on the event queue rather than running it synchronously.

Write the following code in `main`:

```
print('first');

Future(
  () => print('second'),
);

print('third');
```

The constructor of `Future` takes an anonymous function. `Future` then adds that function to the event queue.

Run the code above. This is what you'll get:

```
first
third
second
```

`second` comes last. Why is that? Think about what's happening:

1. Dart always runs the synchronous code first. `print('first')` is synchronous, so Dart executes it immediately on the main isolate.

2. Then Dart comes to `Future`. Dart takes the function inside `Future` and adds it to the event queue. The event queue code has to wait for all the synchronous code to finish before it can go.

3. `print('third')` is also synchronous, so Dart executes that next.
4. Finally, there's no more synchronous code, so Dart takes `print('second')` off the event queue and executes it.

Adding a Task to the Microtask Queue

You'll only need to add a task to the microtask queue once in a blue moon.

Like, literally.

Count how many times you've seen a blue moon in your life. How many did you get? Zero? Yeah, that's about how often you'll need to explicitly put something on the microtask queue in your Dart career. Unless you're writing some low-level library, you can forget about this queue and trust Dart to handle the events there.

However, should the need arise, scheduling tasks on the microtask queue is possible.

Replace the code in `main` with the following:

```
print('first');

Future(
  () => print('second'),
);

Future.microtask(
  () => print('third'),
);

print('fourth');
```

Adding an anonymous function to the `Future.microtask` constructor puts this code on the microtask queue.

Run the code above and check the results:

```
first
fourth
third
second
```

Here's the step-by-step:

1. Dart always runs synchronous code first, so that's why `first` and `fourth` are first.

2. Dart added `print('second')` to the event queue and `print('third')` to the microtask queue.

3. Once the synchronous code finishes, Dart prioritizes any code in the microtask queue. That's why `third` is next.

4. Finally, when the microtask queue is empty, Dart gives the code in the event queue a chance. That's why `second` is last.

Running Synchronous Code After an Event Queue Task

Sometimes you might want to perform a task immediately after a task from the event queue finishes.

Replace the code in `main` with the following:

```
print('first');

Future(
  () => print('second'),
).then(
  (value) => print('third'),
);

Future(
  () => print('fourth'),
);

print('fifth');
```

Here are a few notes:

- The `then` method of a `Future` instance will execute an anonymous function immediately after the future completes. This code is synchronous.
- When futures complete successfully, they return a value. You'll learn more about that in the next chapter. For now, ignore `value` in the `then` callback.
- You'll also learn about `async`/`await` syntax in Chapter 12, "Futures". It's a little easier to use than `then`.

Run the code above. This is what you'll see:

```
first
fifth
second
third
fourth
```

By now, you should know why `first` and `fifth` are first. They're both synchronous, and synchronous code always goes first. `second` and `fourth` both get added to the event queue, but because `then` runs its code synchronously after `second` finishes, `third` jumps in before `fourth` has a chance to come off the event queue.

Intentionally Delaying a Task

Sometimes, it's useful to simulate a long-running task. You can accomplish this with `Future.delayed`. Dart will add a task to the event queue after some time.

Replace the contents of `main` with the following code:

```
print('first');

Future.delayed(
  Duration(seconds: 2),
  () => print('second'),
);

print('third');
```

`Future.delayed` takes two parameters. The first is the duration of time you want to wait before starting the task. The second is the function you want to run after completing the duration. Dart adds the function to the event queue at that point.

Run the code above. First, you only see the following:

```
first
third
```

But two seconds later, Dart adds `second` to the list:

```
first
third
second
```

By the time the duration passed, all the synchronous code was long finished, so `print('second')` didn't have to wait very long on the event queue. Dart executed it right away.

Is this all starting to make sense? If not, the challenge below and its accompanying explanation should help you.

Challenge

Before moving on, here's a challenge to test your understanding of how Dart handles asynchronous tasks. An explanation follows the challenge, but try to figure out the solution yourself before looking.

Challenge 1: What Order?

In what order will Dart print the numbered statements? Why?

```
void main() {
  print('1 synchronous');
  Future(() => print('2 event queue')).then(
    (value) => print('3 synchronous'),
  );
  Future.microtask(() => print('4 microtask queue'));
  Future.microtask(() => print('5 microtask queue'));
  Future.delayed(
    Duration(seconds: 1),
    () => print('6 event queue'),
  );
  Future(() => print('7 event queue')).then(
    (value) => Future(() => print('8 event queue')),
  );
  Future(() => print('9 event queue')).then(
    (value) => Future.microtask(
      () => print('10 microtask queue'),
    ),
  );
  print('11 synchronous');
}
```

Write your answer down before reading the solution that follows.

Solution to Challenge 1

For brevity, the explanations below will refer to each task by its number. For example, `print('1 synchronous')` is abbreviated as 1.

Step 0

```
void main() {
  // ...
}
```

Dart creates the main isolate and calls your `main` function:

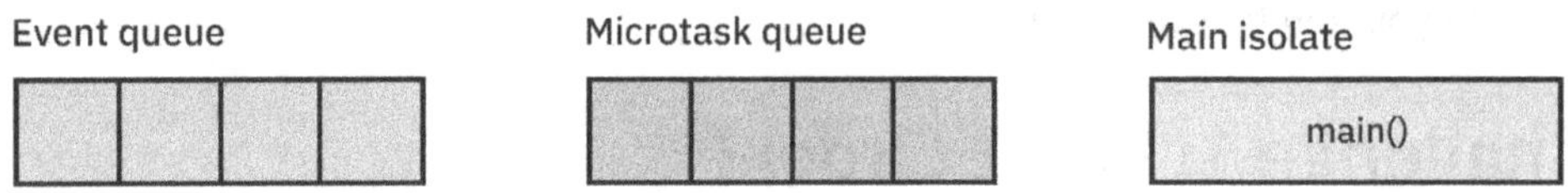

Step 1

```
print('1 synchronous');
```

1 is synchronous, so Dart executes it immediately in the main isolate:

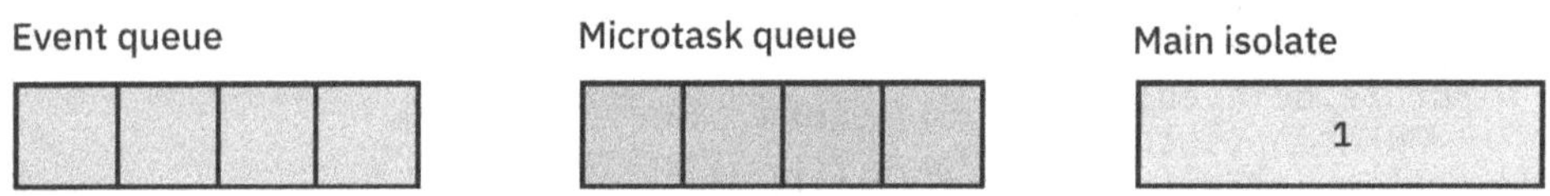

Step 2

```
Future(() => print('2 event queue')).then(
  (value) => print('3 synchronous'),
);
```

Dart adds 2 to the event queue.

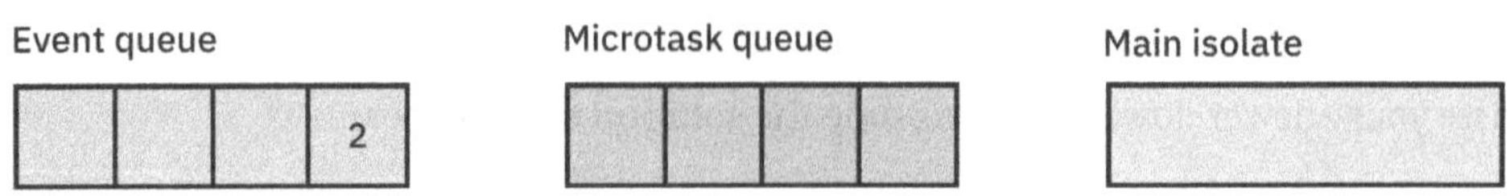

Step 3

```
Future.microtask(() => print('4 microtask queue'));
```

Dart adds 4 to the microtask queue:

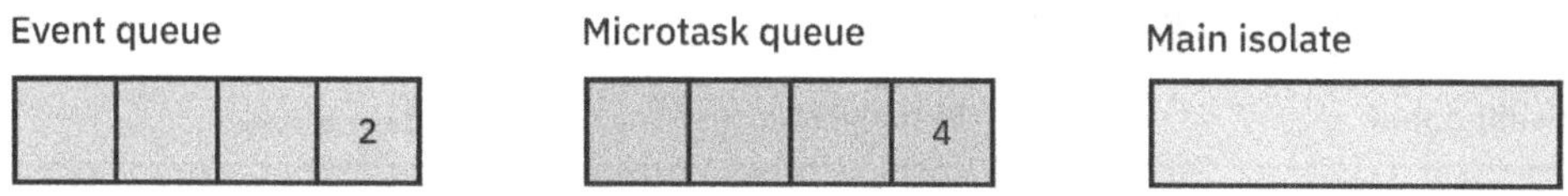

Step 4

```
Future.microtask(() => print('5 microtask queue'));
```

Dart adds 5 to the microtask queue:

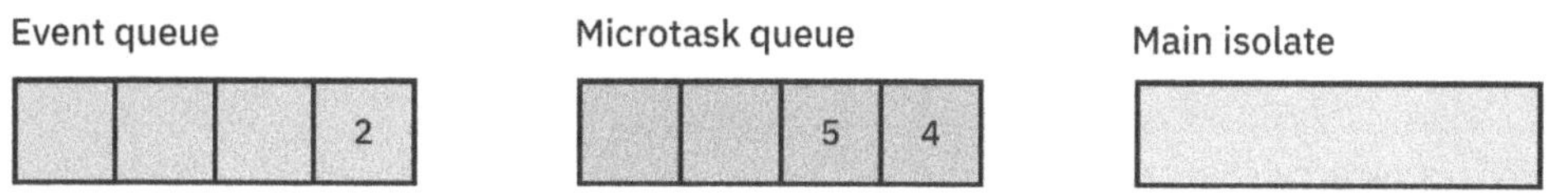

Step 5

```
Future.delayed(
  Duration(seconds: 1),
  () => print('6 event queue'),
);
```

Dart starts an internal timer for one second. The queues remain unchanged:

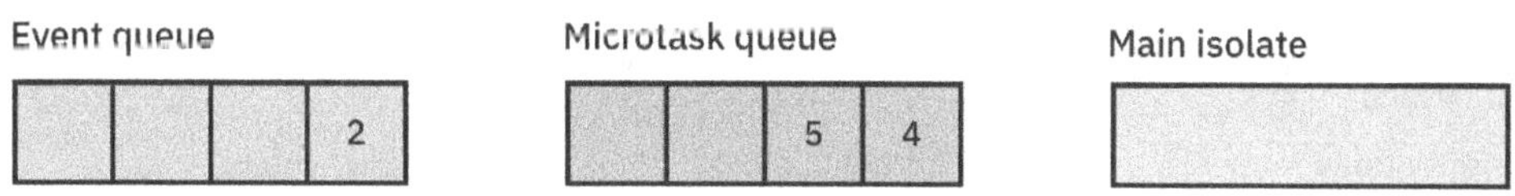

Step 6

```
Future(() => print('7 event queue')).then(
  (value) => Future(() => print('8 event queue')),
);
```

Dart adds 7 to the event queue:

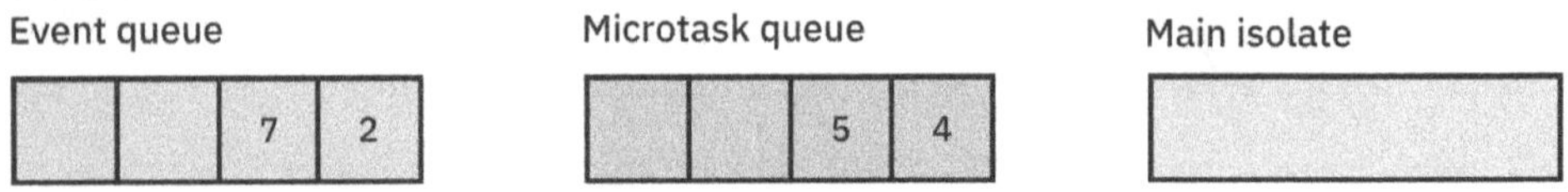

Step 7

```
Future(() => print('9 event queue')).then(
  (value) => Future.microtask(
    () => print('10 microtask queue'),
  ),
);
```

Dart adds 9 to the event queue:

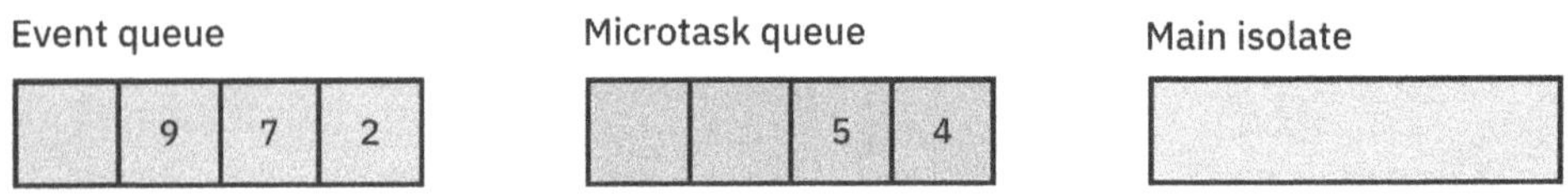

Step 8

```
print('11 synchronous');
```

11 is synchronous, so Dart executes it immediately:

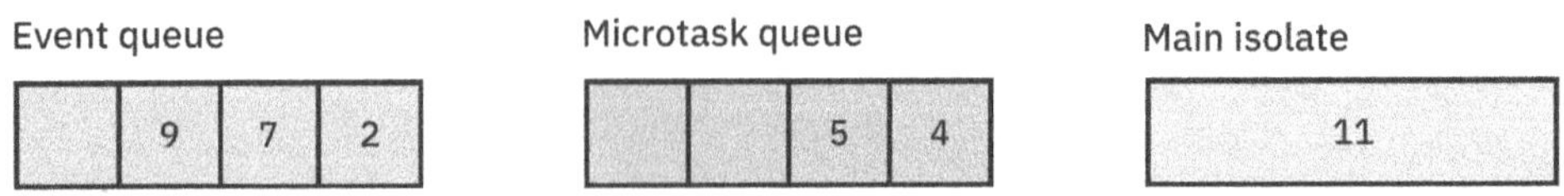

Step 9

```
print('4 microtask queue');
```

All the synchronous tasks have finished, so Dart executes the first task in the microtask queue:

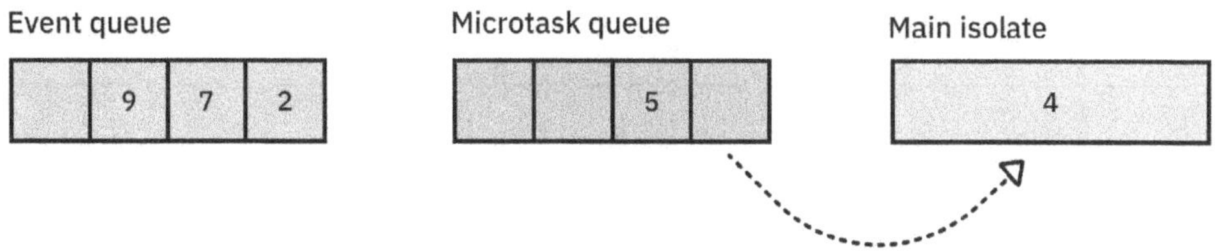

Step 10

```
print('5 microtask queue');
```

Dart then executes the next task in the microtask queue:

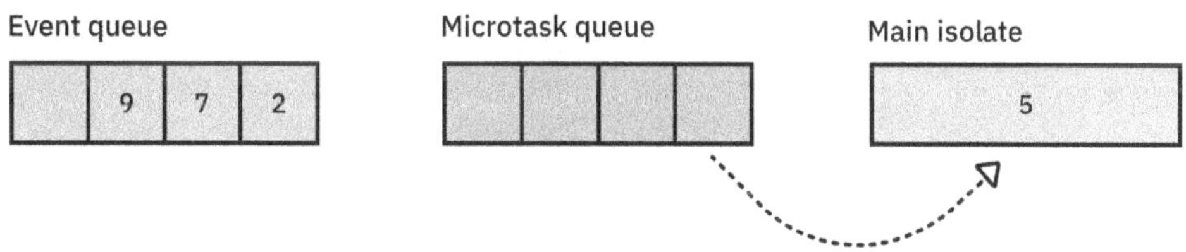

Step 11

```
print('2 event queue');
```

The microtask queue is empty now, so Dart takes the first task off of the event queue and executes it in the main isolate:

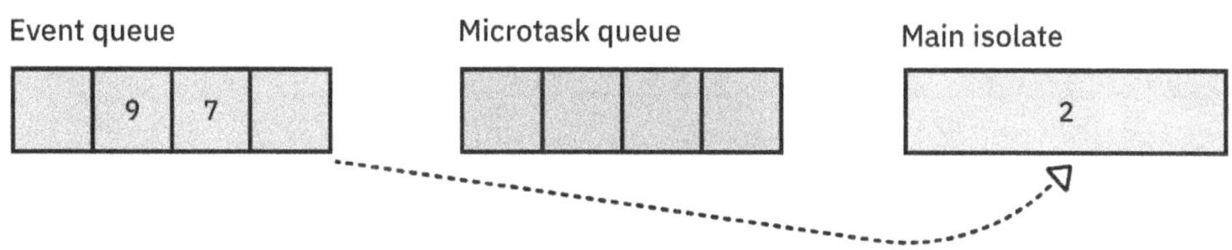

Step 12

```
Future(() => print('2 event queue')).then(
  (value) => print('3 synchronous'),
);
```

As soon as 2 finishes, Dart executes 3 synchronously:

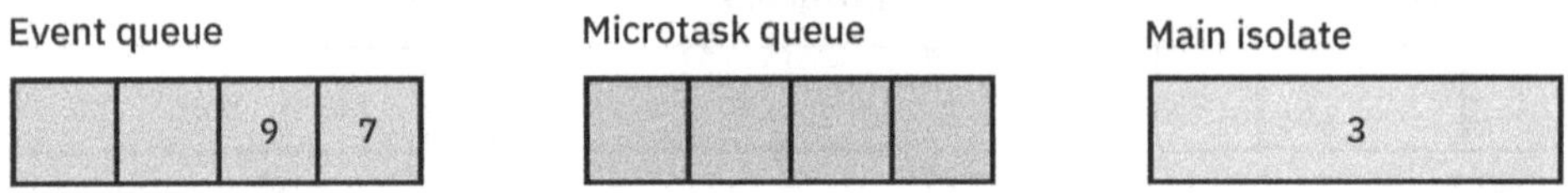

Step 13

```
print('7 event queue');
```

Dart takes 7 off of the event queue and executes it:

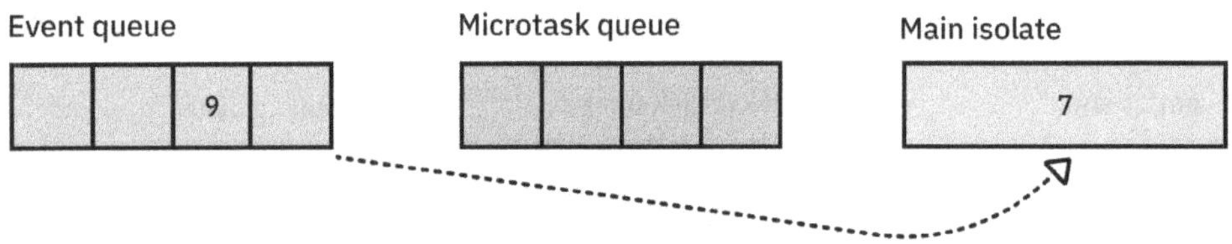

Step 14

```
Future(() => print('7 event queue')).then(
  (value) => Future(() => print('8 event queue')),
);
```

When 7 finishes, Dart schedules 8 at the end of the event queue:

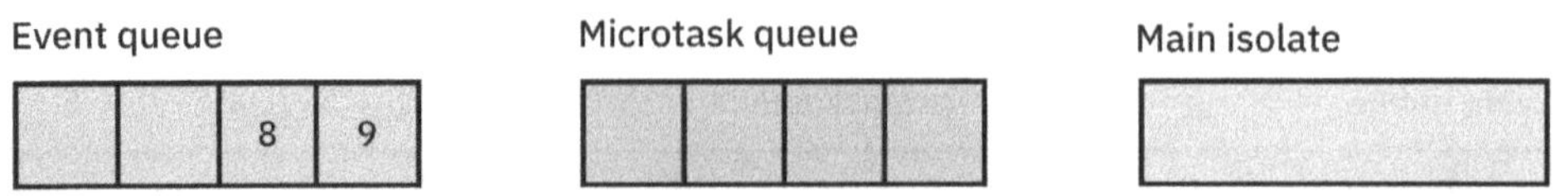

Step 15

```
print('9 event queue');
```

Dart takes `9` off of the event queue and executes it:

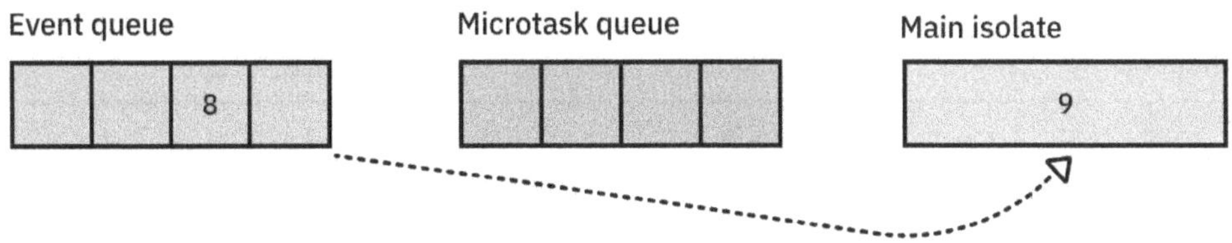

Step 16

```
Future(() => print('9 event queue')).then(
  (value) => Future.microtask(
    () => print('10 microtask queue'),
  ),
);
```

When `9` finishes, Dart adds `10` to the microtask queue:

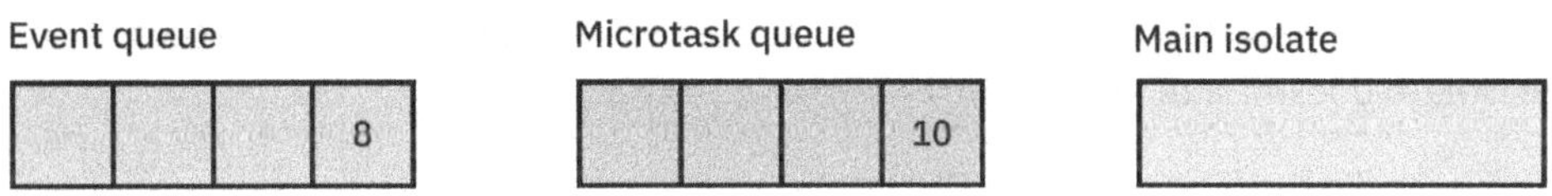

Step 17

```
print('10 microtask queue');
```

The microtask queue has priority over the event queue, so Dart executes `10` before `8`:

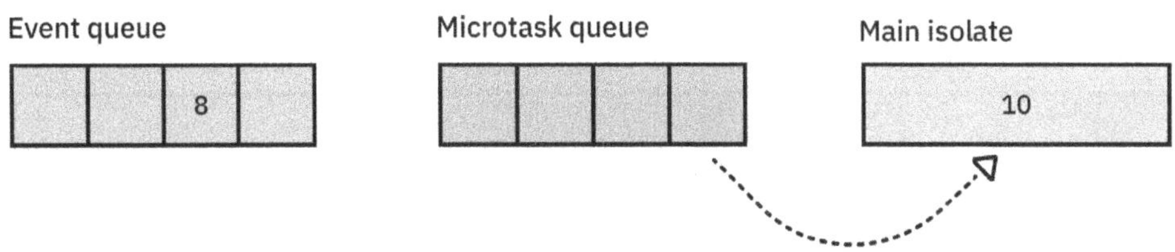

Step 18

```
print('8 event queue');
```

The microtask queue is empty now, so Dart takes 8 off of the event queue and executes it:

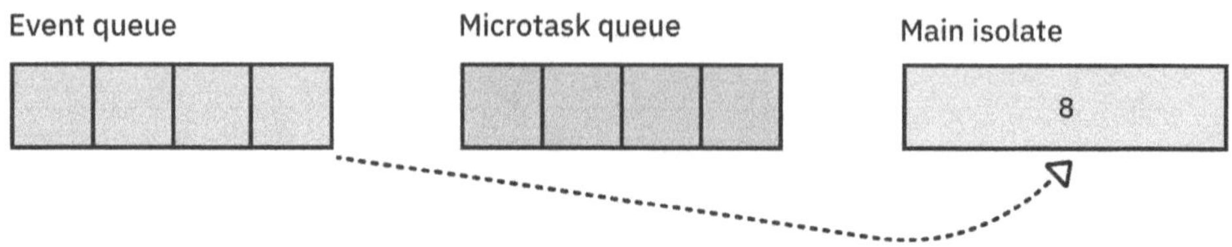

Step 19

The queues are all empty now:

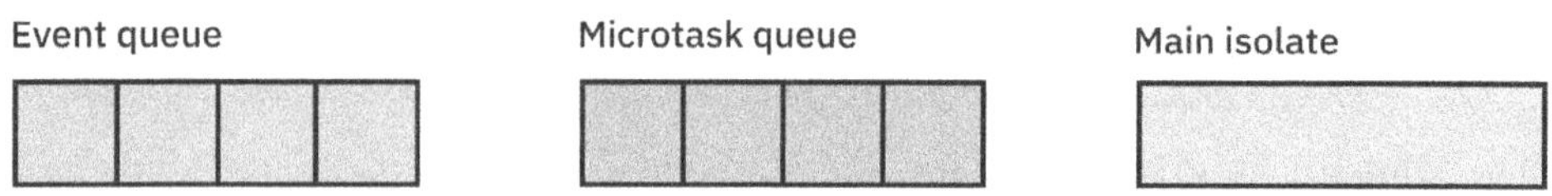

However, Dart is still waiting on the `Future.delayed` timer it set back in Step 5, so the isolate doesn't exit yet.

Step 20

```
Future.delayed(
  Duration(seconds: 1),
  () => print('6 event queue'),
);
```

Sometime later, the duration finally completes, so Dart adds 6 to the event queue:

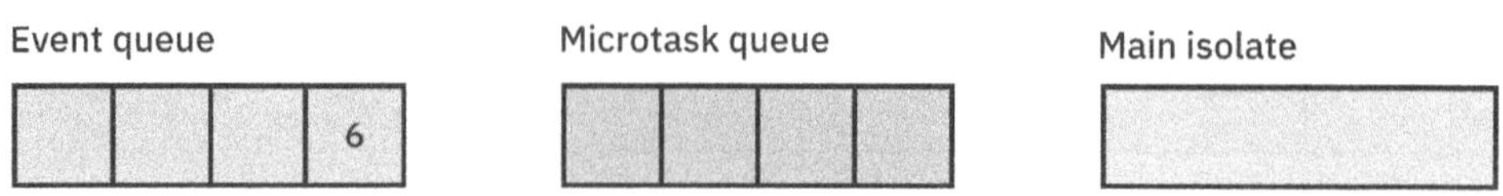

Step 21

```
print('6 event queue');
```

There's nothing to wait for, so Dart takes 6 off the event queue and executes it:

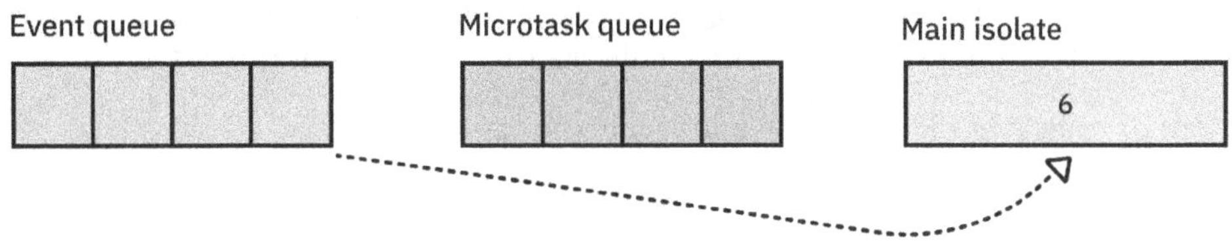

Step 22

The queues are all empty again:

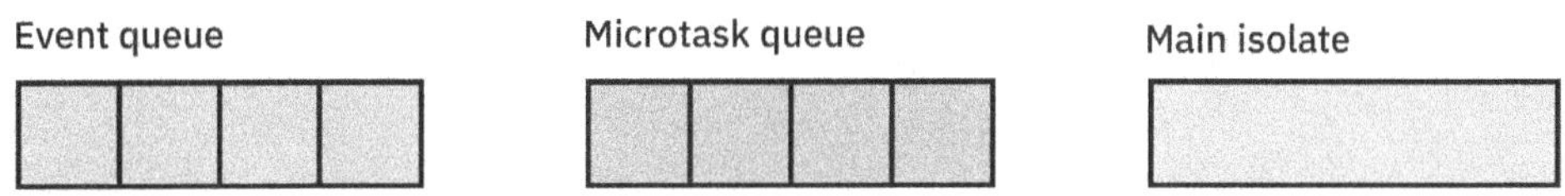

Dart isn't waiting for anything either, so the isolate exits and the application terminates.

Result

Here is the final output:

```
1 synchronous
11 synchronous
4 microtask queue
5 microtask queue
2 event queue
3 synchronous
7 event queue
9 event queue
10 microtask queue
8 event queue
6 event queue
```

If you wrote down the correct answer, give yourself a well-deserved pat on the back!

Key Points

- Dart is single-threaded and handles asynchronous programming through concurrency rather than parallelism.
- Concurrency refers to rescheduling tasks to run later on the same thread, whereas parallelism refers to running tasks simultaneously on different threads.
- Dart uses an event loop to schedule asynchronous tasks
- The event loop has an event queue and a microtask queue.
- A queue is a first-in-first-out (FIFO) data structure.
- Synchronous code always runs first and cannot be interrupted. After this comes anything in the microtask queue, and when these finish, any tasks in the event queue.
- You can run code in parallel by creating a new isolate.

Where to Go From Here?

You learned about queues as first-in-first-out data structures in this chapter. If you'd like to learn more, as well as how to build a queue, check out the "Queues" chapter in *Data Structures & Algorithms in Dart*.

Chapter 12: Futures

By Jonathan Sande

You've got dishes to wash, phone calls to return, clothes to dry and emails to write... *aaaand* you'll get to them right after watching one more meme video. Why work so hard now when you've got so much time tomorrow?

You're not the only one who's good at procrastination. Dart is also an expert at rescheduling things for the future. In the previous chapter, you learned how Dart handles asynchronous code with its event loop. You also learned how to add tasks to the event and microtask queues using the `Future` class. In this chapter, you'll shift your focus from the internal workings of the event loop and learn some practical uses of working with **futures**. These are asynchronous tasks that complete after some time.

Here are some common examples of tasks that Dart handles asynchronously:

- Making network requests.
- Reading and writing a file.
- Accessing a database.

With each of these, you express your intent to perform the task but have to wait for the task to complete. This chapter will teach you how to make network requests, but the process for handling all these asynchronous operations is similar.

The Future Type

Dart's `Future` type is a promise to complete a task or give you a value in the future. Here's the signature of a function that returns a future:

```
Future<int> countTheAtoms();
```

`Future` itself is generic; it can provide any type. In this case, the future is promising to give you an integer. In your code, if you called `countTheAtoms`, Dart would quickly return an object of type `Future<int>`. In effect, this is saying, "Hey, I'll get back to you with that `int` sometime later. Carry on!", in which case you'd proceed to run whatever synchronous code is next.

Behind the scenes, Dart has passed your request on to, presumably, an atom-counting machine, which runs independently of your main Dart isolate. There's nothing on the event queue at this point, and your main thread is free to do other things. Dart knows about the uncompleted future, though. When the atom-counting machine finishes its work, it tells Dart, which puts the result, along with any code you gave it to handle the result, on the event queue. Dart says, "Sorry that took so long. Who knew there were 9.2 quintillion atoms in that little grain of sand! I'll put your handling code at the end of the event queue. Give the event loop a few milliseconds, and then it'll be your turn."

> **Note**: Because the largest an `int` can be on a 64 bit system is 9,223,372,036,854,775,807, or 2^63 - 1, it would be better to use `BigInt` as the return type of `countTheAtoms`. Although slower, `BigInt` can handle arbitrarily large numbers. When `int` values are too big at compile time, there's a compile-time error. However, at runtime, they overflow — that is, `9223372036854775807 + 1 == -9223372036854775808`.

States for a Future

Before a future completes, there isn't anything you can do with it. But after it completes, it will have two possible results: the value you were asking for or an error. This all works out to three different states for a future:

- Uncompleted.
- Completed with a value.
- Completed with an error.

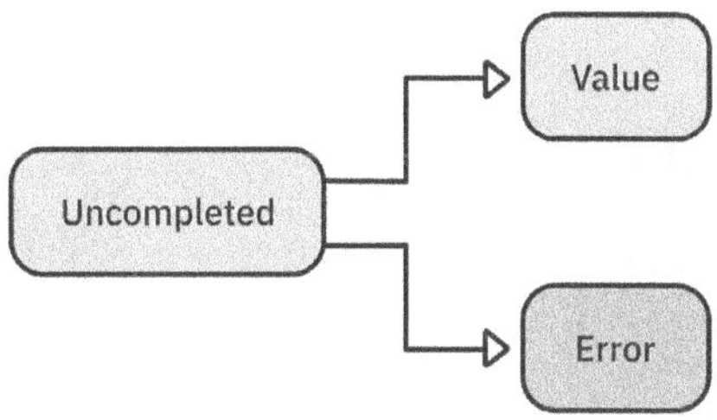

Future states

Example of a Future

One easy way to see a future in action is with the `Future.delayed` constructor. You saw an example of that in the last chapter, so the following is a review:

```
// 1
final myFuture = Future<int>.delayed(
  // 2
  Duration(seconds: 1),
  // 3
  () => 42,
);
```

Here's what's happening:

1. `myFuture` is of type `Future<int>`.
2. The first argument is a `Duration`. After a delay of 1 second, Dart will add the anonymous function in the second argument to the event queue.
3. When the event loop gets to `() => 42`, it will run that function in the main isolate, causing the function to return the integer 42.

In the previous future, the value you want is the 42, but how do you get it? Your variable `myFuture` isn't 42; it's a future that's a promise to return an `int` or an error. You can see that if you try to print `myFuture`:

```
print(myFuture);
```

Run that, and the result is:

```
Instance of 'Future<int>'
```

So how do you access the value? And what if the future completes with an error?

Getting the Results

There are two ways to get at the value after a future completes. One is with callbacks, and the other is with `async-await`.

Using Callbacks

As you learned in Chapter 2, "Anonymous Functions", a **callback** is an anonymous function that will run after some event has completed. In the case of a future, there are three callback opportunities: `then`, `catchError` and `whenComplete`. You used `then` in the last chapter, but you'll see how all three work now.

Replace the body of the `main` function with the following code:

```
print('Before the future');

final myFuture = Future<int>.delayed(
  Duration(seconds: 1),
  () => 42,
)
    .then(
      (value) => print('Value: $value'),
    )
    .catchError(
      (Object error) => print('Error: $error'),
    )
    .whenComplete(
      () => print('Future is complete'),
    );

print('After the future');
```

A future will either give you a value or an error. If it completes with a value, you can get the value by adding a callback to the `then` method. The anonymous function provides the `value` as an argument so you can access it. On the other hand, if the future completes with an error, you can handle it in `catchError`. But regardless of whether the future completes with a value or an error, you can run any final code in `whenComplete`.

Run the code above to see these results:

```
Before the future
After the future
Value: 42
Future is complete.
```

If you worked carefully through Chapter 11, "Concurrency", you weren't surprised that Dart printed "After the future" before the future results. That `print` statement is synchronous, so it ran immediately. Even if the future didn't have a one-second delay, it would still have to go to the event queue and wait for all the synchronous code to finish.

Using Async-Await

Callbacks are pretty easy to understand, but they can be hard to read, especially if you nest them. A more readable way to write the code above is using the `async` and `await` syntax. This syntax makes futures look much more like synchronous code.

Writing the Code

Replace the entire `main` function with the following:

```
// 1
Future<void> main() async {
  print('Before the future');

  // 2
  final value = await Future<int>.delayed(
    Duration(seconds: 1),
    () => 42,
  );
  print('Value: $value');

  print('After the future');
}
```

There are a few changes this time:

1. If a function uses the `await` keyword anywhere in its body, it must return a `Future` and add the `async` keyword before the opening curly brace. Using `async` clearly tells Dart this is an asynchronous function and that the results will go to the event queue. Because `main` doesn't return a value, you use `Future<void>`.
2. In front of the future, you added the `await` keyword. Once Dart sees `await`, the rest of the function won't run until the future completes. If the future completes with a value, there are no callbacks; you have direct access to that value. Thus, the type of the `value` variable above isn't `Future`, but `int`.

Run the code above to see the following results:

```
Before the future
Value: 42
After the future
```

This time, "After the future" gets printed last. That's because *everything* after the `await` keyword is sent to the event queue.

"What if the future returns an error, though?"

For that, use a `try-catch` block.

Handing Potential Errors

You learned about `try-catch` blocks in Chapter 10, "Error Handling". Here's what the future you wrote above looks like inside a `try-catch` block:

```
print('Before the future');

try {
  final value = await Future<int>.delayed(
    Duration(seconds: 1),
    () => 42,
  );
  print('Value: $value');
} catch (error) {
  print(error);
} finally {
  print('Future is complete');
}

print('After the future');
```

The `catch` and `finally` blocks correspond to the `catchError` and `whenComplete` callbacks you saw earlier. If the future completes with an error, Dart will immediately abort the `try` block and call the `catch` block. Error or not, Dart will always call the `finally` block.

Run the code above to see the following result:

```
Before the future
Value: 42
Future is complete
After the future
```

The future finished with a value, so Dart didn't call the `catch` block.

Asynchronous Network Requests

In the examples above, you used `Future.delayed` to simulate a task that takes a long time. Using `Future.delayed` is useful during app development for this reason: You can implement an interface with a mock network request class to see how your UI will react while the app waits for a response.

As useful as `Future.delayed` is, though, eventually, you'll need to implement the real network request class. The following example will show how to make an HTTP request to access a REST API. This example will use many concepts you've learned in the *Dart Apprentice* books.

> **Note**: HTTP, or **hypertext transfer protocol**, is a standard way of communicating with a remote server. REST, or **representational state transfer**, is an architectural style that includes commands like `GET`, `POST`, `PUT` and `DELETE`. The API, or **application programming interface**, is similar in idea to the interfaces you made in Chapter 5, "Interfaces". A remote server defines a specific API using REST commands, which allow clients to access and modify resources on the server.

Creating a Data Class

The web API you'll use will return some data about a to-do list item. The data will be in JSON format. To convert that to a more usable Dart object, you'll create a special class to hold the data. Unsurprisingly, many people call this a **data class**. Such classes usually don't contain many methods because the data is the focus.

Add the following code below the `main` function:

```
class Todo {
  Todo({
    required this.userId,
    required this.id,
    required this.title,
    required this.completed,
  });

  factory Todo.fromJson(Map<String, dynamic> jsonMap) {
    return Todo(
      userId: jsonMap['userId'] as int,
      id: jsonMap['id'] as int,
      title: jsonMap['title'] as String,
      completed: jsonMap['completed'] as bool,
    );
  }

  final int userId;
  final int id;
  final String title;
  final bool completed;

  @override
  String toString() {
    return 'userId: $userId\n'
        'id: $id\n'
        'title: $title\n'
        'completed: $completed';
  }
}
```

Here are a few notes:

- You could have also used a named constructor or a static method instead of a factory constructor for `Todo.fromJson`. Review *Dart Apprentice: Fundamentals* if you need a refresher on classes, constructors and static methods.
- Rather than `dynamic`, you could have written `Object?`. But Dart's JSON decoding library returns `dynamic` values, so it's common to see people use `dynamic` in the `fromJson` input parameter.

Adding the Necessary Imports

The `http` package from the Dart team lets you make a `GET` request to a real server. Make sure your project has a **pubspec.yaml** file, then add the following dependency:

```
dependencies:
  http: ^0.13.5
```

Save the file, and if necessary, run `dart pub get` in the terminal to pull the `http` package from Pub.

Then, at the top of the file with your `main` function, add the following imports:

```
import 'dart:convert';
import 'dart:io';
import 'package:http/http.dart' as http;
```

Here's what each import is for:

- As you recall from Chapter 10, "Error Handling", the `dart:convert` library gives you `jsonDecode`, a function for converting a raw JSON string to a Dart map.
- The `dart:io` library has `HttpException` and `SocketException`, which you'll use shortly.
- The final import is the `http` library you just added to `pubspec.yaml`. Note the `as http` at the end. This isn't necessary, but the `as` keyword lets you prefix any functions from the library with the name `http`. You don't need to call it `http` — any arbitrary name is fine. Feel free to change the name to `pinkElephants` if you so desire. Providing a custom name can be useful for avoiding naming conflicts with other libraries or functions.

Making a GET Request

Now that you have the necessary imports, replace your `main` function with the following code:

```
Future<void> main() async {
  // 1
  final url = 'https://jsonplaceholder.typicode.com/todos/1';
  final parsedUrl = Uri.parse(url);
  // 2, 3
  final response = await http.get(parsedUrl);
  // 4
  final statusCode = response.statusCode;
  if (statusCode != 200) {
    throw HttpException('$statusCode');
  }
  // 5
  final jsonString = response.body;
  dynamic jsonMap = jsonDecode(jsonString);
  // 6
  final todo = Todo.fromJson(jsonMap);
  print(todo);
}
```

There are a few new things here, so have a look at each of them:

1. The URL address is for a server that provides an API that returns sample JSON for developers. It's much like the type of API you would make as a backend for a client app. `Uri.parse` converts the raw URL string to a format that `http.get` recognizes.

2. You use `http.get` to make a `GET` request to the URL. Change `http` to `pinkElephants` if that's what you called it earlier. `GET` requests are the same requests browsers make when you type a URL in the address bar.

3. Because it takes time to contact a server that might exist on another continent, `http.get` returns a future. Dart passes the work of contacting the remote server to the underlying platform, so you won't need to worry about it blocking your app while you wait. Because you're using the `await` keyword, the rest of the main method will be added to the event queue when the future completes. If the future completes with a value, the value will be an object of type `Response`, which includes information from the server.

4. HTTP defines various three-digit status codes. A status code of `200` means `OK` — the request was successful, and the server did what you asked. On the other hand, the common status code of `404` means the server couldn't find what you were asking for. If that happens, you'll throw an `HttpException`.

5. The response body from this URL address includes a string in JSON format. You use `jsonDecode` from the `dart:convert` library to convert the raw JSON string into a Dart map. The type is `dynamic` because JSON strings are untyped by nature. You're assuming that it's a map, but theoretically, it might not be. You can do some extra type checking or error checking if you want to be sure.

6. Once you have a Dart `map`, you can pass it into the `fromJson` factory constructor of your `Todo` class that you wrote earlier.

Make sure you have an internet connection, then run the code above. You'll see a printout from your `Todo` object's `toString` method:

```
userId: 1
id: 1
title: delectus aut autem
completed: false
```

The values of each field come from the remote server.

Handling Errors

A few things could go wrong with the code above, so you'll need to be ready to handle any errors. First, surround all the code inside the body of the `main` function with a `try` block:

```
try {
  final url = 'https://jsonplaceholder.typicode.com/todos/1';
  // ...
}
```

Then, below the `try` block, add the following `catch` blocks:

```
on SocketException catch (error) {
  print(error);
} on HttpException catch (error) {
  print(error);
} on FormatException catch (error) {
  print(error);
}
```

Here's what each of the exceptions means:

- **`SocketException`**: You'll get this exception if there's no internet connection. The `http.get` method is the one to throw the exception.

- **`HttpException`**: You're throwing this exception yourself if the status code isn't `200 OK`.
- **`FormatException`**: `jsonDecode` throws this exception if the JSON string from the server isn't in proper JSON format. It would be unwise to blindly trust whatever the server gives you.

Remember, it's good to be specific in your error-catching. That way, if a different kind of error comes up that you weren't expecting, your app will crash. That allows you to fix the error right away instead of silently ignoring it, as a generic `catch` block would do.

Testing a Socket Exception

Turn off your internet and rerun the code. You should see the following output:

```
SocketException: Failed host lookup:
'jsonplaceholder.typicode.com'
```

In an actual app, instead of just printing a message to the console, you'd probably want to remind the user to turn on their internet.

Turn *your* internet back on and proceed to the next test.

Testing an HTTP Exception

Change the URL to the following:

```
final url = 'https://jsonplaceholder.typicode.com/todos/pink-
elephants';
```

Unless https://jsonplaceholder.typicode.com has recently added the `/pink-elephants` URL endpoint, you'll get a `404` when you rerun the code:

```
HttpException: 404
```

In a real app, you'd inform the user that whatever they were looking for isn't available.

Restore the URL as it was before:

```
final url = 'https://jsonplaceholder.typicode.com/todos/1';
```

You've already had practice throwing a `FormatException` in Chapter 10, "Error Handling", so you can skip that test.

Nice work! You now know how to get the value from a future and handle any errors.

Exercise

1. Use the `Future.delayed` constructor to provide a string after two seconds that says, "I am from the future."
2. Create a `String` variable named `message` that awaits the future to complete with a value.
3. Surround your code with a `try-catch` block.

Creating a Future From Scratch

In the network request example, you simply used the future that the `http` library provided for you. Sometimes, though, you have to create a future from scratch. One example is when you implement an interface that requires a future.

In Chapter 5, "Interfaces", you wrote the following interface:

```
abstract class DataRepository {
  double? fetchTemperature(String city);
}
```

`fetchTemperature` is a synchronous function. However, a real-world app would need to fetch the temperature from a database or web server, so a better interface would return a `Future`. Add the following modified interface to your project:

```
abstract class DataRepository {
  Future<double> fetchTemperature(String city);
}
```

Now, `fetchTemperature` returns a type of `Future<double>` rather than just `double?`. There's no need for the nullable type anymore. The only reason you allowed `null` in the first place was as a default value if there was a problem fetching the temperature. Now that you're using a future, you can just throw an exception if you can't get the temperature.

The problem now is, how do you implement this interface?

If you try to implement it like so:

```
class FakeWebServer implements DataRepository {
  @override
  Future<double> fetchTemperature(String city) {
    return 42.0;
  }
}
```

Dart gives you the following compile-time error:

```
A value of type 'double' can't be returned from the method
'fetchTemperature' because it has a return type of
'Future<double>'.
```

So how do you create a future so you can return it?

There are a few possibilities.

Using the Future Constructor

The most direct way of creating a future is to use one of the constructors of `Future`.

Unnamed Constructor

Replace your `fetchTemperature` implementation in `FakeWebServer` with the following:

```
@override
Future<double> fetchTemperature(String city) {
  return Future(() => 42.0);
}
```

This time `fetchTemperature` returns a future that always completes with a value of `42.0`.

Completing With a Value

Another way to specify that you want the future to complete with a value is to use the `Future.value` named constructor. Replace `fetchTemperature` in `FakeWebServer` with the new form:

```
@override
Future<double> fetchTemperature(String city) {
  return Future.value(42.0);
}
```

`Future.value(42.0)` always completes with a value of `42.0`.

Completing With an Error

Remember that a future can complete with either a value or an error. If you want to return a future that completes with an error, use the `Future.error` named constructor.

Replace `fetchTemperature` with the following implementation:

```
@override
Future<double> fetchTemperature(String city) {
  return Future.error(ArgumentError("$city doesn't exist."));
}
```

When this future completes, it'll give an argument error. This is still your `FakeWebServer` implementation. In a real web server implementation, you would only return the error if there was a problem with the HTTP request.

Giving a Delayed Response

If you were making a Flutter app, it might be nice to wait a while before the future completes so you can see the circular spinner moving for a second or two in the UI. For that, use the `Future.delayed` constructor you've seen previously.

Replace `fetchTemperature` in `FakeWebServer` with the new implementation:

```
@override
Future<double> fetchTemperature(String city) {
  return Future.delayed(
    Duration(seconds: 2),
    () => 42.0,
  );
}
```

This future will complete after two seconds and then return a value.

If you want to return an error instead, throw the error in the callback:

```
@override
Future<double> fetchTemperature(String city) {
  return Future.delayed(
    Duration(seconds: 2),
    () => throw ArgumentError('City does not exist.'),
  );
}
```

This causes the future to complete with an argument error after two seconds.

Using an Async Method

In addition to using the `Future` constructors, an easy way to create a future from scratch is to add the `async` keyword.

Replace your `fetchTemperature` implementation in `FakeWebServer` with the following:

```
@override
Future<double> fetchTemperature(String city) async {
  return 42.0;
}
```

The function directly returns the value `42.0`. But because it contains the `async` keyword, Dart automatically makes the return value a future.

Using a Completer

The previous solutions are fine for most scenarios. However, if you need maximum flexibility, you can use the `Completer` class to create a future.

`Completer` is a part of the `dart:async` library, so first import that at the top of your project file:

```
import 'dart:async';
```

Then, replace your `fetchTemperature` implementation in `FakeWebServer` with the following:

```
@override
Future<double> fetchTemperature(String city) {
  // 1
  final completer = Completer<double>();
  if (city == 'Portland') {
    // 2
    completer.complete(42.0);
  } else {
    // 3
    completer.completeError(ArgumentError("City doesn't
exist."));
  }
  // 4
  return completer.future;
}
```

Here are the steps you take to use the completer:

1. Create a new instance of `Completer`. The future's return value is a `double`, so the completer's generic type is also `double`.

2. You control whether the future will complete with a value or an error. If you want the future to complete with a value, then call `complete` with the value as a parameter.

3. Alternatively, call `completeError` if you want to complete the future with an error.

4. Return the future. In this example, the future has already finished by the time you've reached this point because you're calling `complete` and `completeError` synchronously. You could wrap them in `Future.delayed` if you wanted to see an example of this method returning an uncompleted future.

Testing Your Future Out

Now that you've made your future, you can use it as you would any other future.

Replace `main` with the following code:

```
Future<void> main() async {
  final web = FakeWebServer();
  try {
    final city = 'Portland';
    final degrees = await web.fetchTemperature(city);
    print("It's $degrees degrees in $city.");
  } on ArgumentError catch (error) {
    print(error);
  }
}
```

You're awaiting `fetchTemperature` in this async function. Because `fetchTemperature` might throw an argument error, you wrap it in a `try` block.

Run the code to see the result:

```
It's 42.0 degrees in Portland.
```

That completes the chapter. Knowing how to use futures opens up a whole new world to you. There are many public web APIs you can access to gather data for your apps. Your future has arrived!

Challenges

Before moving on, here are some challenges to test your knowledge of futures. It's best if you try to solve them yourself, but if you get stuck, solutions are available in the **challenge** folder of this chapter.

Challenge 1: Spotty Internet

Implement `FakeWebServer.fetchTemperature` so it completes sometimes with a value and sometimes with an error. Use `Random` to help you.

Challenge 2: What's the Temperature?

Use a real web API to get the temperature and implement the `DataRepository` interface from the lesson.

Free Code Camp (https://www.freecodecamp.org/) has a weather API that takes the following form:

```
https://fcc-weather-api.glitch.me/api/current?
lat=45.5&lon=-122.7
```

You can change the numbers after `lat` and `lon` to specify latitude and longitude for the weather.

Complete the following steps to find the weather:

1. Convert the URL above to a Dart `Uri` object.
2. Use the `http` package to make a GET request. This will give you a `Response` object.
3. Use `response.body` to get the JSON string.
4. Decode the JSON string into a Dart map.
5. Print the map and look for the temperature.
6. Extract the temperature and the city name from the map.
7. Print the weather report as a sentence.
8. Add error handling.

Challenge 3: Care to Make a Comment?

The following link returns a JSON list of comments:

```
https://jsonplaceholder.typicode.com/comments
```

Create a `Comment` data class and convert the raw JSON to a Dart list of type `List<Comment>`.

Key Points

- Using a future, which is of type `Future`, tells Dart that it may reschedule the requested task on the event loop.
- When a future completes, it will contain either the requested value or an error.
- A method that returns a future doesn't necessarily run on a different process or thread. That depends entirely on the implementation.
- You can handle errors from futures with callbacks or `try-catch` blocks.
- You can create a future using a named or unnamed `Future` constructor, returning a value from an `async` method or using a `Completer`.

Where to Go From Here?

If you enjoyed making HTTP requests to access resources from a remote server, you should consider server-side development with Dart. Using a single language for both the front end and the back end is nothing short of amazing. No cognitive switching is required because everything you've learned in this book also applies to writing Dart code on the server.

Chapter 13: Streams

By Jonathan Sande

A future represents a single value that will arrive in the future. On the other hand, a **stream** represents *multiple* values that will arrive in the future. Think of a stream as a list of futures.

You can imagine a stream meandering through the woods as the autumn leaves fall onto the water's surface. Each time a leaf floats by, it's like the value that a Dart stream provides.

Stream of values

Streaming music online rather than downloading the song before playing it is another good comparison. When you stream music, you get many little chunks of data, but when you download the whole file, you get a single value, which is the entire file — a little like what a future returns. The `http.get` command you used in the last section was implemented as a stream internally. However, Dart just waited until the stream finished and then returned all the data at once as a completed future.

Streams, which are of type `Stream`, are used extensively in Dart and Dart-based frameworks. Here are some examples:

- Reading a large file stored locally where new data from the file comes in chunks.
- Downloading a file from a remote server.
- Listening for requests coming into a server.

- Representing user events such as button clicks.
- Relaying changes in app state to the UI.

Although it's possible to build streams from scratch, you usually don't need to do that. You only need to use the streams that Dart or a Dart package provides. The first part of this chapter will teach you how to do that. The chapter will finish by teaching you how to make your own steams.

Using a Stream

Reading and writing files are important skills to learn in Dart. This will also be a good opportunity to practice using a stream.

The `dart:io` library contains a `File` class, which allows you to read data from a file. First, you'll read data the easy way using the `readAsString` method, which returns the file's contents as a future. Then, you'll do it again by reading the data as a stream of bytes.

Adding an Assets File

You need a text file to work with, so you'll add that to your project now.

Create a new folder named **assets** in the root of your project. In that folder, create a file named **text.txt**. Add some text to the file. Although any text will work, *Lorem Ipsum* is a good standby:

```
Lorem ipsum dolor sit amet, consectetur adipiscing elit, sed do
eiusmod tempor incididunt ut labore et dolore magna aliqua. Ut
enim ad minim veniam, quis nostrud exercitation ullamco laboris
nisi ut aliquip ex ea commodo consequat. Duis aute irure dolor
in reprehenderit in voluptate velit esse cillum dolore eu fugiat
nulla pariatur. Excepteur sint occaecat cupidatat non proident,
sunt in culpa qui officia deserunt mollit anim id est laborum.
```

Then, save the file.

> **Note**: *Lorem Ipsum* is often used as filler text by graphic designers and app developers when the meaning of the text doesn't matter. The Latin words were taken from the writings of the Roman statesman and philosopher Cicero but modified to become essentially meaningless.

Reading as a String

Now that you've created the text file, replace your Dart code with the following:

```
import 'dart:io';

Future<void> main() async {
  final file = File('assets/text.txt');
  final contents = await file.readAsString();
  print(contents);
}
```

Here's what's new:

- `File` takes the relative path to your text file as the argument.
- `readAsString` returns `Future<String>`, but by using `await`, you'll receive the string itself when it's ready.

`File` also has a `readAsStringSync` method, which would run synchronously and avoid awaiting a future. However, doing so would block your app if the reading takes a while. Many of the methods on `File` have synchronous versions, but to prevent blocking your app, you should generally prefer the asynchronous versions.

Run the code above, and you'll see the contents of `text.txt` printed to the console.

Increasing the File Size

If the file is large, you can read it as a stream. This allows you to start processing the data more quickly because you don't have to wait to finish reading the entire file as you did in the last example.

When you read a file as a stream, Dart reads the file in chunks. The size of the chunks depends on how Dart is implemented on the system you're using, but it's probably 65,536 bytes per chunk as it was on the local machines used when writing this chapter. The `text.txt` file with *Lorem Ipsum* that you created earlier is only 445 bytes, so trying to stream that file would be no different than simply reading the whole thing as you did before.

To get a text file large enough to stream in chunks, create a new file in the **assets** folder called **text_long.txt**. Copy the *Lorem Ipsum* text and paste it in **text_long.txt** as new lines so that there are 1000 *Lorem Ipsum* copies. You can, of course, select all and recopy from time to time, unless you find it therapeutic to paste things a thousand times. Save the file, and you're ready to proceed.

Alternatively, you can find **text_long.txt** in the **assets** folder of the **final** project that comes with this chapter.

Reading From a Stream

Replace the contents in the body of the `main` function with the following code:

```
final file = File('assets/text_long.txt');
final stream = file.openRead();
stream.listen(
  (data) {
    print(data.length);
  },
);
```

Here are a few points to note:

- Instead of calling `readAsString` on `file`, this time you're calling `openRead`, which returns an object of type `Stream<List<int>>`. That's a lot of angle brackets, but `Stream<List<int>>` simply means it's a stream that periodically produces a list, and that list is a list of integers. The integers are the byte values, and the list is the chunk of data being passed in.
- To subscribe for notifications whenever new data comes in the stream, you call `listen` and pass it an anonymous function that takes a single parameter. The `data` parameter here is of type `List<int>`, which gives you access to the chunk of data coming in from the file.
- Because each integer in the list is one byte, calling `data.length` will tell you the number of bytes in the chunk.

> **Note**: By default, only a single object can listen to a stream. This is known as a **single-subscription stream**. If you want more than one object to be notified of stream events, you need to create a **broadcast stream**, which you could do like so:
>
> ```
> final broadcastStream = stream.asBroadcastStream();
> ```

Run the code in `main`, and you'll see something like the following:

```
65536
65536
65536
65536
```

```
65536
65536
52783
```

At least on the computer used while writing this chapter, the data was all in 65,536-byte chunks until the final one, which was smaller because it didn't quite fill up the 65,536-byte buffer size. Your final chunk might be a different size than the one shown here, depending on how therapeutic your copy-and-paste session was.

Using an Asynchronous For-Loop

Just as you can use callbacks or `async-await` to get the value of a future, you also have two ways to get the values of a stream. In the example above, you used the `listen` callback. Here is the same example using an asynchronous `for` loop:

```
Future<void> main() async {
  final file = File('assets/text_long.txt');
  final stream = file.openRead();
  await for (var data in stream) {
    print(data.length);
  }
}
```

The `await for` keywords cause the loop to pause until the next data event comes in. Run this, and you'll see the same results as before.

Error Handling

Like futures, stream events can also include an error rather than a value.

Stream of values and errors

Be a responsible programmer and plan how to handle errors. Callbacks and `try-catch` blocks both work.

Using a Callback

One way to handle errors is to use the `onError` callback like so:

```
final file = File('assets/text_long.txt');
final stream = file.openRead();
stream.listen(
  (data) {
    print(data.length);
  },
  onError: (Object error) {
    print(error);
  },
  onDone: () {
    print('All finished');
  },
);
```

Here are a couple of points to note:

- When an error occurs, it won't cancel the stream, and you'll continue to receive more data events. If you want to cancel the stream after an error, `listen` also has a `cancelOnError` parameter that you can set to `true`.
- When a stream finishes sending all its data, it'll fire a done event. This gives you a chance to respond with an `onDone` callback.

Using Try-Catch

The other way to handle errors on a stream is with a `try-catch` block in combination with `async-await`. Here is what that looks like:

```
try {
  final file = File('assets/text_long.txt');
  final stream = file.openRead();
  await for (var data in stream) {
    print(data.length);
  }
} on Exception catch (error) {
    print(error);
} finally {
  print('All finished');
}
```

In this example, you're catching all exceptions. A more robust solution would check for specific errors like `FileSystemException`, which Dart would throw if the file didn't exist.

Run either the callback version or the try-catch version, and you'll see the same chunk sizes as before, with the additional text "All finished" printed at the end.

Change the filename to something nonexistent, like pink_elephants.txt, and rerun the code. Confirm that you have a FileSystemException.

```
FileSystemException: Cannot open file, path = 'assets/
pink_elephants.txt' (OS Error: No such file or directory, errno
= 2)
All finished
```

Even with the exception, the finally block (or onDone callback if that's what you used) still printed "All finished".

Cancelling a Stream

As mentioned above, you may use the cancelOnError parameter to tell the stream that you want to stop listening in the event of an error. But even if there isn't an error, you should always cancel your subscription to a stream if you no longer need it. This allows Dart to clean up the memory the stream was using. Failing to do so can cause a memory leak.

Replace your Dart code with the following version:

```
import 'dart:async';
import 'dart:io';

void main() {
  final file = File('assets/text_long.txt');
  final stream = file.openRead();
  StreamSubscription<List<int>>? subscription;
  subscription = stream.listen(
    (data) {
      print(data.length);
      subscription?.cancel();
    },
    cancelOnError: true,
    onDone: () {
      print('All finished');
    },
  );
}
```

Calling `listen` returns a `StreamSubscription`, which is part of the `dart:async` library. Keeping a reference to that in the `subscription` variable allows you to cancel the subscription whenever you want. In this case, you cancel it after the first data event.

Run the code, and you'll only see `65536` printed once. The `onDone` callback was never called because the stream never completed.

Transforming a Stream

Being able to transform a stream as the data is coming in is very powerful. In the examples above, you never did anything with the data except print the length of the bytes list. Those bytes represent text, though, so you're going to transform the data from numbers to text.

For this demonstration, there's no need to use a large text file, so you'll switch back to the 445-byte version of *Lorem Ipsum* in **text.txt**.

Viewing the Bytes

Replace the contents of `main` with the following code:

```
final file = File('assets/text.txt');
final stream = file.openRead();
stream.listen(
  (data) {
    print(data);
  },
);
```

Run that, and you'll see a long list of bytes in decimal form:

```
[76, 111, 114, 101, ... ]
```

Although different computers encode text files using different encodings, the abbreviated list above is from a computer that uses UTF-8 encoding. You might recall that UTF-16 uses 16-bit, or 2-byte, code units to encode Unicode text. UTF-8 uses one to four 8-bit code units to encode Unicode text. Because for values of 127 and below, UTF-8 and Unicode code points are the same, English text only takes one byte per letter. This makes file sizes smaller than UTF-16 encoding. The smaller size helps when saving to disk or sending data over a network.

If you look up 76 in Unicode, you see that it's the capital letter **L**, 111 is **o**, and on it goes with `Lorem ipsum dolor sit...`.

32		48	0	64	@	80	P	96	`	112	p
33	!	49	1	65	A	81	Q	97	a	113	q
34	"	50	2	66	B	82	R	98	b	114	r
35	#	51	3	67	C	83	S	99	c	115	s
36	$	52	4	68	D	84	T	100	d	116	t
37	%	53	5	69	E	85	U	101	e	117	u
38	&	54	6	70	F	86	V	102	f	118	v
39	'	55	7	71	G	87	W	103	g	119	w
40	(	56	8	72	H	88	X	104	h	120	x
41	)	57	9	73	I	89	Y	105	i	121	y
42	*	58	:	74	J	90	Z	106	j	122	z
43	+	59	;	75	K	91	[	107	k	123	{
44	,	60	<	76	L	92	\	108	l	124	|
45	-	61	=	77	M	93	]	109	m	125	}
46	.	62	>	78	N	94	^	110	n	126	~
47	/	63	?	79	O	95	_	111	o	127	DEL

Unicode characters in the range 32-127

Decoding the Bytes

Next, you'll take the UTF-8 bytes and convert them to a string.

Make sure you have the following imports and `main` method:

```
import 'dart:convert';
import 'dart:io';

Future<void> main() async {
  final file = File('assets/text.txt');
  final byteStream = file.openRead();
  final stringStream = byteStream.transform(utf8.decoder);
  await for (var data in stringStream) {
    print(data);
  }
}
```

The main difference here is that you're using `transform`. This method takes the input from the original stream, transforms it with a `StreamTransformer` and outputs a new stream, which you can listen to or loop over as before. In this case, the stream transformer was the `dart:convert` library's `utf8.decoder`, which takes a list of bytes and converts them to a string.

Run the code, and you'll see the *Lorem Ipsum* passage printed in plain text.

Exercise

The following code produces a stream that outputs an integer every second and stops after the tenth time.

```
Stream<int>.periodic(
  Duration(seconds: 1),
  (value) => value,
).take(10);
```

1. Set the stream above to a variable named `myStream`.
2. Use `await for` to print the value of the integer on each data event coming from the stream.

Creating Streams From Scratch

You've learned how to use streams. As you advance in your skills, you might want to also create packages with streams for other developers to use.

Say, for example, you're writing an audio player plugin. You need to take the events that the underlying platform provides and pass them on to Dart. Using a stream is a natural choice for continuous events like playback state changes or the current play position. Because the data comes from outside of Dart, though, you have to create the stream yourself. The rest of this chapter will show you how to do that.

You can create a stream in a few ways:

- Using `Stream` constructors.
- Using asynchronous generators.
- Using stream controllers.

You'll start with constructors and move on to the other methods.

Using Stream Constructors

The `Stream` class has several constructors you can use to create streams. You saw an example in the exercise above with `Stream.periodic`, which added data at periodic intervals. Here are a few more named constructors:

- **`Stream.empty`**: A stream with no values or errors. It's done as soon as you listen to it.
- **`Stream.value`**: A stream with a single value.
- **`Stream.error`**: A stream with a single error.
- **`Stream.fromFuture`**: Converts a future to a stream.
- **`Stream.fromFutures`**: Converts multiple futures to a stream.
- **`Stream.fromIterable`**: Converts an iterable collection to a stream.

Feel free to try them all out. The example below will demonstrate building a stream with the `fromFutures` constructor.

First, create a few futures by replacing the contents of `main` with the following code:

```
final first = Future(() => 'Row');
final second = Future(() => 'row');
final third = Future(() => 'row');
final fourth = Future.delayed(
  Duration(milliseconds: 300),
  () => 'your boat',
);
```

Now, create your stream and listen to it like so:

```
final stream = Stream<String>.fromFutures([
  first,
  second,
  third,
  fourth,
]);

stream.listen((data) {
  print(data);
});
```

`fromFutures` consolidates all your futures into a single stream.

> **Note**: Be sure to add the comma after the last future in the list so they're formatted vertically. That way, they go gently down the stream. :]

Run your code, and there you have it:

```
Row
row
row
your boat
```

Using Asynchronous Generators

The `Stream` constructors are good when they match the data you have, but if you want more flexibility, consider using an asynchronous generator.

A **generator** is a function that produces multiple values in a sequence. As you may recall, Dart has two types of generators: synchronous and asynchronous.

Reviewing Synchronous Generators

You learned about synchronous generators in Chapter 15, "Iterables", of *Dart Apprentice: Fundamentals*. But to review, a **synchronous generator** returns its values as an iterable. These values are available on demand. You can get them as soon as you need them. That's why they're called *synchronous*.

Here's an example of a synchronous generator function that provides the squares of all the integers from 1 to 100 as an iterable:

```
Iterable<int> hundredSquares() sync* {
  for (int i = 1; i <= 100; i++) {
    yield i * i;
  }
}
```

Recall that `sync*`, read "sync star", is what defines the function as a synchronous generator and that `yield` provides the values to the iterable.

By comparison, an **asynchronous generator** returns its values as a stream. You can't get them whenever you want. You have to wait for them. That's why it's called *asynchronous*.

Implementing an Asynchronous Generator

When creating an asynchronous generator, use the `async*` keyword, which you can read as "async star".

> **Note**: It's easy to forget the difference between `async` and `async*`. Here's a reminder: Functions with `async` return *futures*, and functions with `async*` return *streams*.

Add the following top-level function to your project file:

```
Stream<String> consciousness() async* {
  final data = ['con', 'scious', 'ness'];
  for (final part in data) {
    await Future<void>.delayed(Duration(milliseconds: 500));
    yield part;
  }
}
```

Here's what's happening in the stream of `consciousness`:

...this is an async* *function, so the function returns a stream, and like synchronous functions, this function also uses the* yield *keyword to return values in the stream, but unlike synchronous functions, you don't get all the values on demand, so here you're waiting for 500 milliseconds every time you loop because the data here is just simulating data you might get from a database or the user's device or the web or something...*

Listening to the Stream

Replace the contents of `main` with the following:

```
final stream = consciousness();

stream.listen((data) {
  print(data);
});
```

`consciousness` gives you the stream, which you listen to in the usual way.

Run that, and you'll see the following text written to the console one line every half second:

```
con
scious
ness
```

Using Stream Controllers

The final way you'll create a stream is with the low-level `StreamController`. You could go even more low-level than that, but a stream controller is fine for most practical purposes.

Before diving into the code, it would help to understand how streams work.

Understanding Sinks and Streams

The way to add data or errors to a stream is with what's called a **sink**. You can think of this like your kitchen sink with water flowing out of it into a pipe. The water pipe is like a stream. Throwing a grape into the sink is like adding a data value event to the stream. The grape gets washed through the sink's drain and enters the water stream flowing through the pipe. Alternatively, you could throw a cherry in the sink, and it will have the same fate as the grape. Putting in a cherry is like adding an error event. You can also close the sink. Think of that like putting a plug in the hole. No more data or errors can enter the stream.

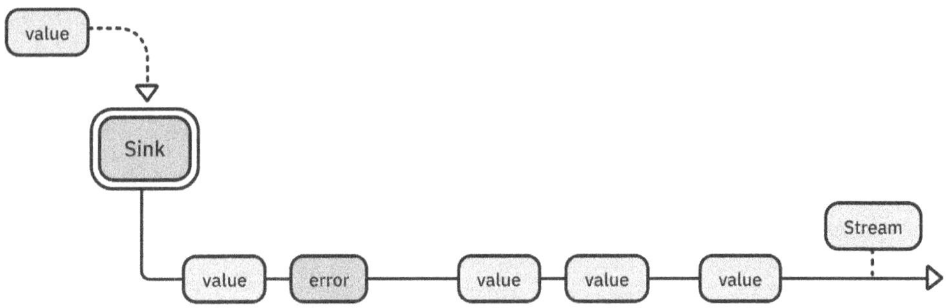

Because adding data and errors are events, a sink is also called an **event sink**.

When you use a stream controller, it creates and manages the sink and stream internally.

Writing the Code

Replace the contents of `main` with the following code:

```
// 1
final controller = StreamController<String>();
final stream = controller.stream;
final sink = controller.sink;
// 2
stream.listen(
```

```
    (value) => print(value),
    onError: (Object error) => print(error),
    onDone: () => print('Sink closed'),
  );
  // 3
  sink.add('grape');
  sink.add('grape');
  sink.add('grape');
  sink.addError(Exception('cherry'));
  sink.add('grape');
  sink.close();
```

Here's what you're doing:

1. Create a stream controller of type `String`. Internally, the controller will take care of creating a string stream and also a sink.
2. Listen for and handle data, error and done events on the stream.
3. Add some data values and errors to the sink. These will flow into the stream. Finally, close the sink. `sink` is of type `StreamSink`, which implements `EventSink`. The `EvenSink` interface ensures you have the `add`, `addError` and `close` methods.

> **Note**: The example above provides a single-subscriber stream. If you need a broadcast stream, use `StreamController<String>.broadcast()`. This allows you to listen to the stream more than once.

Testing It Out

Run your code, and you'll see the following lines in the console:

```
grape
grape
grape
Exception: cherry
grape
Sink closed
```

It works! As you can see, even the low-level solution wasn't very difficult to implement.

If you were making a library package for other people to use, you would probably make the stream controller and the sink private. Just expose the stream to the library users. See the solution to Challenge 2 for an example.

Challenges

Before going on to the next chapter, here are some challenges to test your knowledge of streams. It's best if you try to solve them yourself, but if you get stuck, solutions are available in the **challenge** folder of this chapter.

Challenge 1: Data Stream

The following code uses the `http` package to stream content from the given URL:

```
final url = Uri.parse('https://kodeco.com');
final client = http.Client();
final request = http.Request('GET', url);
final response = await client.send(request);
final stream = response.stream;
```

Your challenge is to transform the stream from bytes to strings and see how many bytes each data chunk is. Add error handling, and when the stream finishes, close the client.

Challenge 2: Heads or Tails?

Create a coin flipping service that provides a stream of 10 random coin flips, each separated by 500 milliseconds. You use the service like so:

```
final coinFlipper = CoinFlippingService();

coinFlipper.onFlip.listen((coin) {
  print(coin);
});

coinFlipper.start();
```

`onFlip` is the name of the stream.

Key Points

- A stream, which is of type `Stream`, is like a series of futures.
- Using a stream enables you to handle data events as they happen rather than waiting for them all to finish.
- You can handle stream errors with callbacks or `try-catch` blocks.
- You can create streams with `Stream` constructors, asynchronous generators or stream controllers.
- A sink is an object for adding values and errors to a stream.

Where to Go From Here?

Streams are powerful, and you can do much more with them. For example, if your app has a "Download Song" button, you don't want to overload the server when some happy kid presses the button as fast as they can a million times. You can consolidate that stream of button-press events into a single server request. This is called **debouncing**. It doesn't come built into Dart, but packages like RxDart (https://pub.dev/packages/rxdart) support debouncing and many other stream functions.

Chapter 14: Isolates

By Jonathan Sande

Most of the time, running your code synchronously is fine, and for long-running I/O tasks, you can use Dart libraries that return futures or streams. But sometimes, you might discover your code is too computationally expensive and degrades your app's performance. That's when you should offload that code to a separate thread so it can run in parallel.

As you recall from Chapter 11, "Concurrency", the way to achieve parallelism in Dart is to create a new **isolate**. Isolates are so named because their memory and code are isolated from the outside world. An isolate's memory isn't accessible from another isolate, and each isolate has its own thread for running Dart code in an event loop. The only way to communicate from one isolate to another is through message passing. Thus, when a worker isolate finishes a task, it passes the results back to the main isolate as a message.

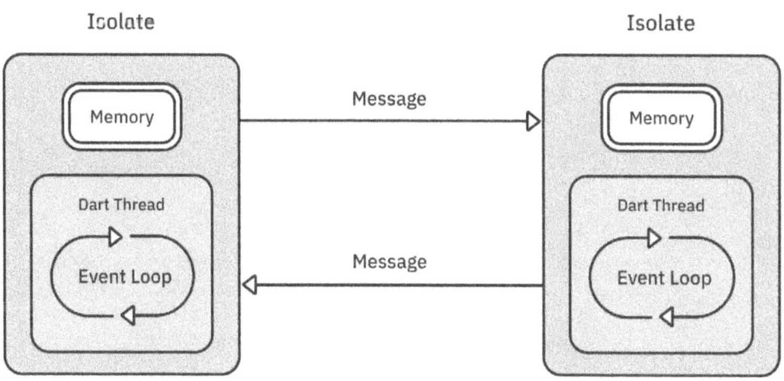

The description above is fine from the developer's perspective. That's all you need to know. The internal implementation, though, is somewhat more complex. When you create a new isolate, Dart adds it to an **isolate group**. The isolate group shares resources between the isolates, so creating a new isolate is fast and memory efficient. This includes sharing the available memory, also called a **heap**. Isolates still can't modify the mutable objects in other isolates, but they can share references to the same immutable objects. In addition to sharing the heap, isolate groups have helper threads to work with all the isolates. This is more efficient than performing these tasks separately for each isolate. An example of this is garbage collection.

> **Note**: Dart manages memory with a process known as **garbage collection**. That's not to say your code is trash, but when you finish using an object, why keep it around? It's like all those pictures you drew when you were 5. Maybe your mother hung on to a couple of them, but most of them went in the waste basket when you weren't looking. Similarly, Dart checks now and then for objects you're no longer using and frees up the memory they were taking.

Unresponsive Applications

Doing too much work on the main isolate will make your app appear janky at best and completely unresponsive at worst. This can happen with both synchronous and asynchronous code.

App-Stopping Synchronous Code

First, look at some synchronous code that puts a heavy load on the CPU.

Add the following code as a top-level function to your project:

```
String playHideAndSeekTheLongVersion() {
  var counting = 0;
  for (var i = 1; i <= 10000000000; i++) {
    counting = i;
  }
  return '$counting! Ready or not, here I come!';
}
```

Counting to 10 billion takes a while — even for a computer. If you run that function in a Flutter app, your app's UI will freeze until the function finishes.

Run the function now from the body of main like so:

```
print("OK, I'm counting...");
print(playHideAndSeekTheLongVersion());
```

Unless you have a *reeeeally* nice computer, you'll notice a significant pause until the counting finishes. That was the CPU doing a lot of work.

App-Stopping Asynchronous Code

If you've finished Chapter 11, "Concurrency", and Chapter 12, "Futures", you should know that making the function asynchronous doesn't fix the problem.

Replace playHideAndSeekTheLongVersion with the following asynchronous implementation:

```
Future<String> playHideAndSeekTheLongVersion() async {
  var counting = 0;
  await Future(() {
    for (var i = 1; i <= 10000000000; i++) {
      counting = i;
    }
  });
  return '$counting! Ready or not, here I come!';
}
```

Run that using await:

```
Future<void> main() async {
  print("OK, I'm counting...");
  print(await playHideAndSeekTheLongVersion());
}
```

Another long wait. That would be a quick uninstall followed by a one-star rating if it happened on your phone app.

Adding the computationally intensive loop as an anonymous function in a Future constructor makes it a future. However, think about what's going on here. Dart simply puts that anonymous function at the end of the event queue. True, all the events before it will go first, but once the 10-billion-counter-loop gets to the end of the queue, it'll start running synchronously and block the app until it finishes. Using a future only delays the eventual block.

One-Way Isolate Communication

When you're accustomed to using futures from the Dart I/O libraries, it's easy to get lulled into thinking that futures always run in the background, but that's not the case. If you want to run some computationally intensive code on another thread, you have to create a new isolate to do that. The term for creating an isolate in Dart is called **spawning**.

Since for all practical purposes isolates don't share any memory, they can only communicate by sending messages. To send a message, you need a send port and a receive port. Picture a **receive port** like an audio speaker that listens for messages and plays them when they come. Every receive port has a **send port**, which you can picture as a microphone connected by a long cord back to the receive port. Message communication happens only in one direction. You send messages with the send port and listen to them with the receive port. There's no way to use the receive port to send messages to the send port.

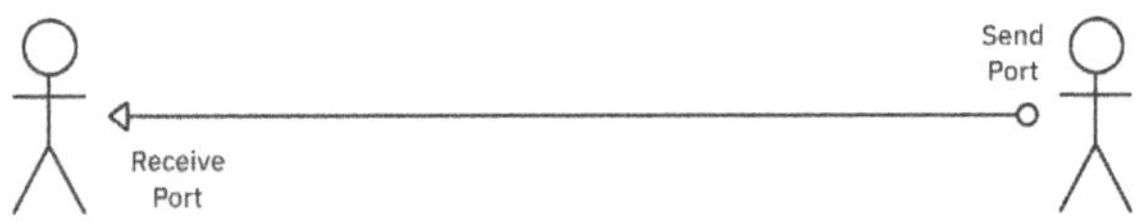

Normally, before you spawn a new isolate, you first create a `ReceivePort` object. Then, when you spawn the isolate, you pass it a reference to the `SendPort` property of your receive port. That way, the new isolate can send messages over the send port back to the main isolate's receive port.

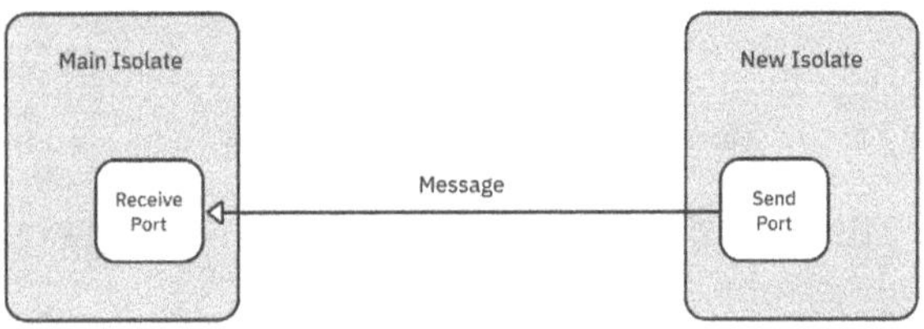

This type of one-way communication is useful for one-off tasks. You give an isolate some work to do, and when it's finished, it returns the result over the send port.

Here are some examples where one-way communication is fine:

- Decoding JSON.
- Performing a scientific calculation.
- Processing an image.

In the next section, you'll move your hide-and-seek function over to an isolate. This will demonstrate the steps you need to take when spawning an isolate and setting up the communication ports.

Using a Send Port to Return Results

Before you create a new isolate, you need to write the first function the isolate will run. This function is called the **entry point**. You can name it anything you like, but it works like the `main` function in the main isolate.

You'll modify `playHideAndSeekTheLongVersion` to run as the entry-point function on the new isolate. You must pass any result that this function computes back over a send port. You can't just return it directly from the function. That means you need to pass in the send port as an argument.

`SendPort` is part of the `dart:isolate` library, so import that first:

```
import 'dart:isolate';
```

Replace your previous implementation of `playHideAndSeekTheLongVersion` with the following:

```
// 1
void playHideAndSeekTheLongVersion(SendPort sendPort) {
  var counting = 0;
  for (var i = 1; i <= 1000000000; i++) {
    counting = i;
  }
  final message = '$counting! Ready or not, here I come!';
  // 2
  Isolate.exit(sendPort, message);
}
```

Here are a couple of comments:

1. This time, you have a `void` function with a `SendPort` parameter.
2. Calling `Isolate.exit` sends your message over the send port and then shuts the isolate down.

Spawning the Isolate and Listening for Messages

You've finished preparing the code that your new isolate will run. Now, you have to create the isolate itself.

Replace `main` with the following code:

```
Future<void> main() async {
  // 1
  final receivePort = ReceivePort();

  // 2
  await Isolate.spawn<SendPort>(
    // 3
    playHideAndSeekTheLongVersion,
    // 4
    receivePort.sendPort,
  );

  // 5
  final message = await receivePort.first as String;
  print(message);
}
```

Here's what you did:

1. You created a receive port to listen for messages from the new isolate.
2. Next, you spawned a new isolate and gave it two arguments. Specifying `SendPort` as the generic type tells Dart the type of the entry-point function parameter.
3. The first argument of `Isolate.spawn` is the entry-point function. That function must be a top-level or static function. It must also take a single argument.
4. The second argument of `Isolate.spawn` is the argument for the entry-point function. In this case, it's a `SendPort` object.
5. `ReceivePort` implements the `Stream` interface, so you can treat it like a stream. Calling `await receivePort.first` waits for the first message coming in the stream and then cancels the stream subscription. `playHideAndSeekTheLongVersion` only sends a single message; that's all you need to wait for.

Run the code above, and after a pause, you'll see the following output:

```
1000000000! Ready or not, here I come!
```

You counted to only a billion this time, so the pause was shorter. Because this was done on another isolate, though, even 10 billion wouldn't freeze your app's UI.

> **Note**: Flutter has a highly simplified way of starting a new isolate, performing some work and then returning the result using a function called `compute`. Rather than passing the function a send port, you just pass it any needed values. In this case, you could just pass it the number to count to:
>
> `await compute(playHideAndSeekTheLongVersion, 1000000000);`

Sending Multiple Messages

The previous example showed how to send a single message from the worker isolate to the parent isolate. You can modify that example to send multiple messages.

Replace `playHideAndSeekTheLongVersion` with the following code:

```
void playHideAndSeekTheLongVersion(SendPort sendPort) {
  sendPort.send("OK, I'm counting...");

  var counting = 0;
  for (var i = 1; i <= 1000000000; i++) {
    counting = i;
  }

  sendPort.send('$counting! Ready or not, here I come!');
  sendPort.send(null);
}
```

Note the following points:

- `SendPort.send` is the way to send a message over the send port. Calling it three times means you send three messages.
- This time, you don't shut down the isolate here. Instead, you send `null` as a signal that you're finished. `null` doesn't need to be your signal. You could also send the string `'done'` or `'finished'`. You just have to agree on the signal with the main isolate that's listening.

> **Note**: In addition to strings and `null`, Dart allows you to send almost any data type with `SendPort.send` as long as you're sending a message to another isolate in the same isolate group. This even includes user-defined data types like `User` or `Person`, but it comes with some restrictions. For example, you can't send `Socket` or `ReceivePort` objects. If the isolate is in a different isolate group, which you can create using the `Isolate.spawnUri` constructor, you can send only a few basic data types.
>
> Dart sends immutable objects like strings by reference, which makes passing them very fast. Mutable objects, on the other hand, are copied. That can take longer for large objects with many properties which in turn have other properties. For example, `person` might include properties like `person.home.address` and `person.job.duties`.

Next, replace the body of `main` with the following code:

```
final receivePort = ReceivePort();

final isolate = await Isolate.spawn<SendPort>(
  playHideAndSeekTheLongVersion,
  receivePort.sendPort,
);

receivePort.listen((Object? message) {
  if (message is String) {
    print(message);
  } else if (message == null) {
    receivePort.close();
    isolate.kill();
  }
});
```

Because `receivePort` is a stream, you can listen to it like any other stream. If the message is a string, you just print it. But if the message is `null`, that's your signal to close the receive port and shut down the isolate.

Run the code, and you'll see:

```
OK, I'm counting...
1000000000! Ready or not, here I come!
```

Passing Multiple Arguments When Spawning an Isolate

The function `playHideAndSeekTheLongVersion` in the example above only took a single parameter of type `SendPort`. What if you want to pass in more than one argument? For example, it might be nice to specify the integer you want to count to.

An easy way to accomplish this is to make the function parameter a list or a map instead of a send port. Then, you can make the first element the send port and add as many other elements as you need for additional arguments.

Replace `playHideAndSeekTheLongVersion` with the following modification:

```
void playHideAndSeekTheLongVersion(List<Object> arguments) {
  final sendPort = arguments[0] as SendPort;
  final countTo = arguments[1] as int;

  sendPort.send("OK, I'm counting...");

  var counting = 0;
  for (var i = 1; i <= countTo; i++) {
    counting = i;
  }

  sendPort.send('$counting! Ready or not, here I come!');
  sendPort.send(null);
}
```

The parameter now is `List<Object> arguments`. This isn't quite as readable as having separately named parameters, but it allows you to pass in as many arguments as you like. With a list, you access the arguments by index. Your code assumes that `arguments[0]` is the send port and `arguments[1]` is the integer you're counting to.

> **Note**: If you want to use a map instead, write `Map<String, Object> arguments` as the function parameter. Then, you could extract the send port with `arguments['sendPort']` and the integer with `arguments['countTo'];`. This offers the advantage of being somewhat more readable than `arguments[0]` and `arguments[1]`.

You've updated the entry-point function, but you also must modify how you create the isolate.

Replace the `isolate` assignment in `main` with the following version:

```
final isolate = await Isolate.spawn<List<Object>>(
  playHideAndSeekTheLongVersion,
  [receivePort.sendPort, 999999999],
);
```

Here are the differences:

- The generic type of `spawn` is now `List<Object>` instead of `SendPort`.
- The second parameter of spawn is a list, where the first element is the send port and the second element is the value to count to.

Rerun the code, and you should see the new result:

```
OK, I'm counting...
999999999! Ready or not, here I come!
```

Two-Way Isolate Communication

One-way communication is fine for single tasks, but sometimes you might need to keep an isolate around for a while.

Here are some examples of long-running tasks where two-way communication may be necessary:

- Communicating with a game server.
- Decoding multiple JSON files.
- Handling server clients.

For two-way communication, both sides need a send port and a receive port:

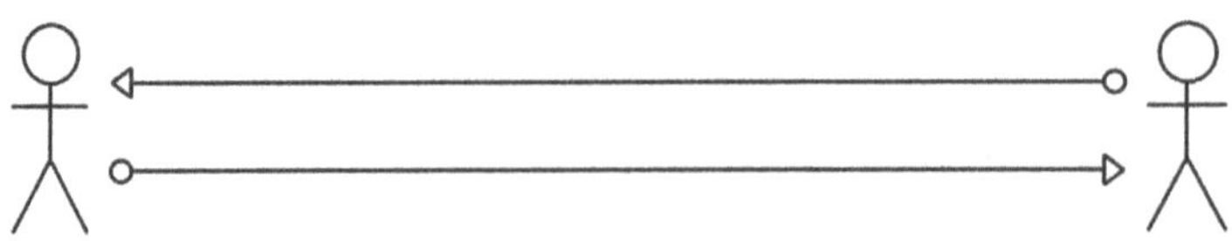

Two-way communication isn't built into isolates by default, but you can set it up in a two-step process:

1. Create a receive port in the parent isolate and pass its send port to the child isolate. This allows the child to send messages to the parent.

2. Create a receive port in the child isolate and send that receive port's send port back to the parent isolate. This allows the parent to send messages to the child.

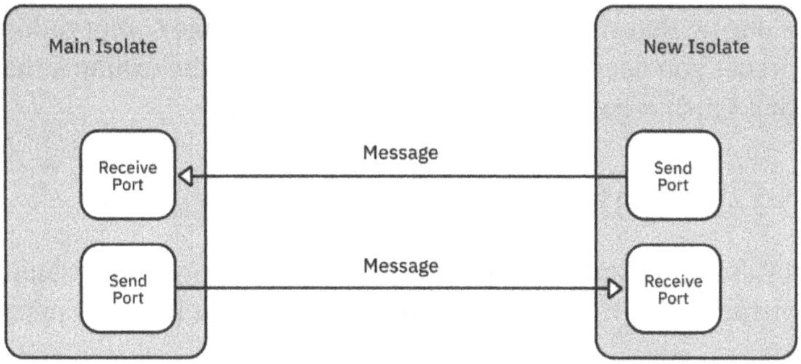

The sections below will guide you through setting up two-way communication. In the example, Earth will represent the main or parent isolate, and Mars will represent the worker or child isolate. The example will demonstrate two-way communication as Earth and Mars communicate back and forth.

Defining the Work

You'll start by creating a class with methods that perform some work. Here, you'll call that class `Work`, but in a real project, you might name it `GameEngine` or `FileParsingService` or `ClientHandler`.

Add the following import to your project file:

```
import 'dart:io';
```

This will give you access to the `sleep` function, which you'll use below.

Add the following class to your project file:

```
class Work {
  Future<int> doSomething() async {
    print('doing some work...');
    sleep(Duration(seconds: 1));
    return 42;
  }

  Future<int> doSomethingElse() async {
    print('doing some other work...');
    sleep(Duration(seconds: 1));
    return 24;
  }
}
```

You can use both `sleep` and `Future.delayed` to pause your program. But `sleep` is synchronous, so it will block all execution of other code for the full duration you specify. If you used it in an app with a user interface, your app would become unresponsive during that time. Here, `sleep` represents some computationally intensive task that you need to run on another isolate. In the example that follows, this is work that Earth requires but is offloading to Mars.

Creating an Entry Point for an Isolate

You'll begin by creating your entry-point function. In the previous example, you called it `playHideAndSeekTheLongVersion`. This time you'll simply name it `_entryPoint`.

First, make sure you still have the `dart:isolate` import at the top of the project file:

```
import 'dart:isolate';
```

Then, add the following entry point as a top-level function:

```
// 1
Future<void> _entryPoint(SendPort sendToEarthPort) async {
  // 2
  final receiveOnMarsPort = ReceivePort();
  sendToEarthPort.send(receiveOnMarsPort.sendPort);
  // 3
  final work = Work();

  // TODO: add listener
}
```

This is what you've got so far:

1. `sendToEarthPort` is the send port that belongs to Earth's receive port. The Mars isolate can use this port to send messages back to the Earth isolate.
2. In the second step of setting up two-way communication, you create a receive port in the child isolate and send its send port back to the parent isolate. Thus, the first "message" you send back to Earth is `receiveOnMarsPort.sendPort`.
3. You create an instance of `Work` inside `_entryPoint`. Now, you're ready to perform your heavy work on the Mars isolate.

The diagram below pictures what you're trying to accomplish. You've begun setting up the ports on the Mars side, and you'll create the Earth ports later.

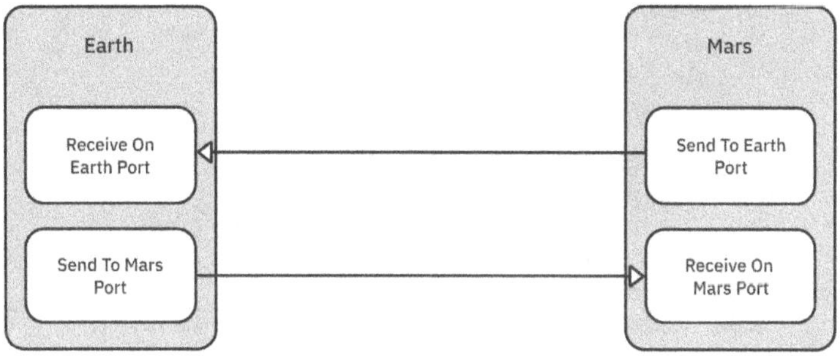

Listening for Messages from the Parent Isolate

A receive port is a stream, so you can listen to `receiveOnMarsPort` to respond to messages from Earth.

Replace the comment `// TODO: add listener` from above with the following listener:

```
receiveOnMarsPort.listen((Object? messageFromEarth) async {
  // 1
  await Future<void>.delayed(Duration(seconds: 1));
  print('Message from Earth: $messageFromEarth');
  // 2
  if (messageFromEarth == 'Hey from Earth') {
    sendToEarthPort.send('Hey from Mars');
  }
  else if (messageFromEarth == 'Can you help?') {
    sendToEarthPort.send('sure');
  }
  // 3
  else if (messageFromEarth == 'doSomething') {
    final result = await work.doSomething();
    // 4
    sendToEarthPort.send({
      'method': 'doSomething',
      'result': result,
    });
  }
  else if (messageFromEarth == 'doSomethingElse') {
    final result = await work.doSomethingElse();
    sendToEarthPort.send({
      'method': 'doSomethingElse',
      'result': result,
    });
    sendToEarthPort.send('done');
  }
});
```

These points correspond to the numbered comments in the code:

1. It takes at least five minutes for messages from Earth to reach Mars in real life. Pausing for a second here will make the final result feel a bit like interplanetary communication.

2. Depending on the message from Earth, you can respond in different ways. And because you have Earth's send port, you can send messages back to Earth.

3. Generally, what you'll do when you listen to messages from the parent isolate is to map some string message to its corresponding method on your worker class. For example, you match the string `'doSomething'` to the method `work.doSomething` and `'doSomethingElse'` to `work.doSomethingElse`. This is a more realistic scenario than saying, "Hey".

4. When these tasks have completed, you pass the result back to Earth over its send port. Remember that these methods will complete asynchronously. Including the method name in the message will help Earth know which method call this is coming from.

Preparing to Create the Child Isolate

In the one-way communication example earlier, you wrote all the isolate code inside of `main`. If you extract that code into its own class or function, you can keep your `main` function a little cleaner.

Add the following class to your project:

```
// 1
class Earth {
  // 2
  final _receiveOnEarthPort = ReceivePort();
  SendPort? _sendToMarsPort;
  Isolate? _marsIsolate;

  // TODO: create isolate

  // 3
  void dispose() {
    _receiveOnEarthPort.close();
    _marsIsolate?.kill();
    _marsIsolate = null;
  }
}
```

Here are a few notes:

1. `Earth` encapsulates all your isolate communication code. It represents the main isolate.

2. You've defined a receive port to listen to messages from the Mars child isolate and a send port to send messages back to Mars. Mars will give you this send port later after you've spawned the isolate.

3. When you finish the work on Mars, you can call `dispose` to shut the isolate down and clean up the resources.

Creating the Child Isolate

Now that you've written the supporting code, you're finally ready to create the Mars isolate.

Replace the comment `// TODO: create isolate` above with the following code:

```
Future<void> contactMars() async {
  if (_marsIsolate != null) return;

  _marsIsolate = await Isolate.spawn<SendPort>(
    _entryPoint,
    _receiveOnEarthPort.sendPort,
  );

  // TODO: add listener
}
```

`Isolate.spawn` assigns a value to `_marsIsolate`. You provide the Mars `_entryPoint` function with a send port as an argument.

Listening for Messages From the Child Isolate

Next, you must listen and respond to messages from your Mars isolate.

Replace the comment `// TODO: add listener` above with the following listener on the `_receiveOnEarthPort` stream:

```
_receiveOnEarthPort.listen((Object? messageFromMars) async {
  await Future<void>.delayed(Duration(seconds: 1));
  print('Message from Mars: $messageFromMars');
  // 1
  if (messageFromMars is SendPort) {
    _sendToMarsPort = messageFromMars;
    _sendToMarsPort?.send('Hey from Earth');
  }
  // 2
  else if (messageFromMars == 'Hey from Mars') {
    _sendToMarsPort?.send('Can you help?');
  }
  else if (messageFromMars == 'sure') {
    _sendToMarsPort?.send('doSomething');
    _sendToMarsPort?.send('doSomethingElse');
  }
  // 3
  else if (messageFromMars is Map) {
    final method = messageFromMars['method'] as String;
    final result = messageFromMars['result'] as int;
    print('The result of $method is $result');
```

```
  }
  // 4
  else if (messageFromMars == 'done') {
    print('shutting down');
    dispose();
  }
});
```

Here's what's happening:

1. Recall that the first message you sent back to Earth from Mars was the send port for Mars' receive port. Thus, the first message you receive in this message stream should be of type `SendPort`. This is your messaging link to Mars, so save a reference to it in `_sendToMarsPort`.
2. Respond to messages from Mars. You can't directly call functions in the Mars isolate, but you can send strings that will trigger function calls. You've already mapped those strings to their respective functions when you wrote `_entryPoint` earlier.
3. Because you can't directly call functions, you also don't directly get a function's return value. However, you can listen for a message you know takes the form of a return value. In the case of `_entryPoint`, you defined the return value to be of type `Map` where the keys are `method` and `result`. As you've seen, maps and lists are useful when you want to pass multiple values.
4. The isolate sends a message that it's all finished with its work now, so you can shut it down.

> **Note**: As an alternative, you could use a `StreamQueue` rather than calling `listen` on the receive port stream. This would make the code easier to read in some ways. The example here didn't use it, because that would have required more background explanation. `StreamQueue` is worth looking into, though.

Running Your Code

Everything is set up now, so you're ready to see if it works.

Replace `main` with the following:

```
Future<void> main() async {
  final earth = Earth();
  await earth.contactMars();
}
```

Run your code, and you should see the following exchange take place in one-second increments as your main isolate on Earth communicates with the Mars isolate:

```
Message from Mars: SendPort
Message from Earth: Hey from Earth
Message from Mars: Hey from Mars
Message from Earth: Can you help?
Message from Mars: sure
Message from Earth: doSomething
doing some work...
Message from Earth: doSomethingElse
doing some other work...
Message from Mars: {method: doSomething, result: 42}
The result of doSomething is 42
Message from Mars: {method: doSomethingElse, result: 24}
The result of doSomethingElse is 24
Message from Mars: done
shutting down
```

Note that the result of `doSomething` doesn't come directly after Earth sends the message, and the same is true for `doSomethingElse`. Isolate communication is inherently asynchronous.

Challenges

Before finishing, here are some challenges to test your knowledge of isolates. It's best if you try to solve them yourself, but if you get stuck, solutions are available in the **challenge** folder of this chapter.

Challenge 1: Fibonacci From Afar

Calculate the nth Fibonacci number. The Fibonacci sequence starts with 1, then 1 again, and then all subsequent numbers in the sequence are simply the previous two values in the sequence added together (1, 1, 2, 3, 5, 8...).

If you worked through the challenges in *Dart Apprentice: Fundamentals*, Chapter 6, "Loops", you've already solved this. Repeat the challenge but run the code in a separate isolate. Pass the value of *n* to the new isolate as an argument and send the result back to the main isolate.

Challenge 2: Parsing JSON

Parsing large JSON strings can be CPU intensive and thus a candidate for a task to run on a separate isolate. The following JSON string isn't particularly large, but convert it to a map on a separate isolate:

```
const jsonString = '''
{
  "language": "Dart",
  "feeling": "love it",
  "level": "intermediate"
}
''';
```

Key Points

- You can run Dart code on another thread by spawning a new isolate.
- Dart isolates don't share any mutable memory state and communicate only through messages.
- You can pass multiple arguments to an isolate's entry-point function using a list or a map.
- Use a `ReceivePort` to listen for messages from another isolate.
- Use a `SendPort` to send messages to another isolate.
- For long-running isolates, you can set up two-way communication by creating a send port and receive port for both isolates.

Where to Go From Here?

You know how to run Dart code in parallel now. As a word of advice, though, don't feel like you need to pre-optimize everything you think might be a computationally intensive task. Write your code as if it will all run on the main isolate. Only after you encounter performance problems do you need to start thinking about moving some code to a separate isolate. Check out the Dart DevTools (https://dart.dev/tools/dart-devtools) to learn more about profiling your app's performance.

One great thing about isolates is that when a child isolate crashes, it doesn't need to bring your whole app down. For example, you could have hundreds or even thousands of separate isolates handling user connections on a server. One malicious user who finds a way to crash the isolate wouldn't affect the other users on the server. Learning how to listen for and handle isolate errors would be a great next step.

15 Conclusion

Congratulations! You've reached the end of *Dart Apprentice: Beyond the Basics*. We hope you've enjoyed reading this book and that the skills you've acquired will help you in all your future Dart projects.

At this point, you can consider yourself a solid intermediate-level developer in the Dart programming language. You understand the principles of object-oriented programming, string manipulation, generics, error handling and asynchronous programming. If you go on to develop Flutter apps or build backend servers in Dart, you shouldn't have any trouble with the language-related aspects of app development.

On your path to becoming an expert Dart developer, here are some topics you might explore next:

- **Flutter**: Read *Flutter Apprentice* from Kodeco.
- **Servers**: Check out `shelf` and other server packages on Pub.
- **Unit testing**: Write tests to ensure your code works as expected.
- **Algorithms**: Read *Data Structures & Algorithms in Dart* from Kodeco.
- **Web sockets**: Learn how real-time communication works.
- **FFI**: Communicate with native C APIs.
- **Bit manipulation**: Work directly with raw byte data.

- **Packages**: Share your code with other developers.
- **Command-line apps**: Build tools you can run in the terminal.
- **Devtools**: Profile your apps to measure their performance and find errors.
- **Databases**: Connect to a database server to save and retrieve data.

Don't know where to start? The best way to learn is by making something useful, so choose frontend development with Flutter or backend development with server-side Dart. After that, learn unit testing. Unit testing is so important that we should probably add a chapter on it in the next edition of this book. After unit testing, let the needs of your Flutter or server app guide you in the next topic of study. Little by little, you'll become proficient in a wide variety of skills.

If you had any questions or comments as you worked through this book, please stop by our forums at https://forums.kodeco.com and look for the particular forum category for this book.

Thank you again for purchasing this book. Your continued support is what makes the books, tutorials, videos and other things we do at Kodeco possible. We truly appreciate it!

– The *Dart Apprentice: Beyond the Basics* team

www.ingramcontent.com/pod-product-compliance
Lightning Source LLC
Chambersburg PA
CBHW061206240926
51846CB00006B/1125
9781950325788